EARTH
TO
TABLE
EVERY
DAY

ALSO BY THE AUTHORS

EARTH TO TABLE: SEASONAL RECIPES FROM AN ORGANIC FARM

EARTH TO TABLE EVERY DAY

COOKING *with* GOOD INGREDIENTS
THROUGH *the* SEASONS

JEFF CRUMP *and* BETTINA SCHORMANN

PENGUIN

an imprint of Penguin Canada, a division of Penguin Random House Canada Limited

Canada • USA • UK • Ireland • Australia • New Zealand • India • South Africa • China

First published 2018

www.penguinrandomhouse.ca

LIBRARY AND ARCHIVES CANADA CATALOGUING IN PUBLICATION

Crump, Jeff, author
        Earth to table every day : cooking with good ingredients through the seasons / Jeff Crump and Bettina Schormann.

Issued in print and electronic formats.
ISBN 978-0-7352-3348-5 (hardcover).—ISBN 978-0-7352-3349-2 (electronic)

        1. Seasonal cooking. 2. Cooking. 3. Cookbooks. I. Schormann, Bettina, author II. Title.

TX714.C78 2018   641.5'64   C2017-907393-1
                                                                 C2017-907394-X

Cover and interior design by Lisa Jager
Cover images by Maya Visnyei
Food styling by Claire Stubbs
Prop styling by Catherine Doherty

Printed and bound in China

10 9 8 7 6 5 4 3 2 1

PEARLE
HOSPITALITY

Penguin
Random House
PENGUIN CANADA

For our partner, Aaron Ciancone,
and to the memory of his father,
Ron Ciancone, a true lover of good food
and its power to bring people together.

CONTENTS

BREADS

INSPIRATION: CHAD ROBERTSON, TARTINE BAKERY, SAN FRANCISCO, CALIFORNIA | 12

SOUPS

TO EVERY SEASON | 26

SALADS

DIGGING IN THE DIRT | 46

SHARED APPETIZERS
PASS THE BREAD, PLEASE | 82

Blistered Padrón Peppers with Basil and Pine Nut
    Mayonnaise | 85
Grilled Octopus with Potatoes and Mint | 86
Toast Four Ways | 89
Devils on Horseback | 92
General Tso's Fried Cauliflower | 95

Crispy Brussels Sprouts with Umami Sauce | 96
Fried Calamari | 99
Mushroom Tarts with Taleggio Cheese | 100
Creamy Hummus with Fried Chickpeas | 103
Burrata and Blistered Cherry Tomatoes | 104

BURGERS AND SANDWICHES
FUN IN THE KITCHEN | 108

Cheese Burger | 111
Umami Burger | 112
Quinoa Super-Star Veggie Burger | 115
Lamb Burger | 116
Porchetta Sandwich | 119
Marinated Chickpea Sandwich with
    Romesco Sauce | 121
Japanese Tuna Salad Sandwich | 122

Avocado, Tomato, Chicken, and Bacon
    Sandwich | 124
Crispy Eggplant Melt | 127
Fried Chicken Sandwich | 128
Pear and Prosciutto Sandwich | 131
Tomato, Goat Cheese, and Caramelized Onion
    Tartine | 132

PIZZAS
INSPIRATION: NANCY SILVERTON, PIZZERIA MOZZA, LOS ANGELES, CALIFORNIA | 136

Pizza Dough | 139
Margherita Pizza | 140
Apple Bacon Pizza | 143
Goat Cheese and Bacon Pizza | 144
Bee Sting Pizza | 147
Butter Chicken Pizza | 148

Green Goddess Pizza | 149
Roasted Mushroom Pizza | 150
Cheese Louise Pizza | 153
The Rob Pizza | 154
Vampire Slayer Pizza | 157
Wise Guy Pizza | 158

MAINS

PASTRY AND DESSERTS

STAPLES

OUR STORY

The steel town of Hamilton, Ontario, was where we became friends and colleagues, and where we found the creative space and support to fashion an earth-to-table experience that set us apart and started us on our inevitable course towards building our first restaurant, Earth to Table: Bread Bar. (We refer to it, in this cookbook as in life, simply as Bread Bar.) In 2005, as the executive chef and the pastry chef at a local establishment called the Ancaster Mill, we started hunting for farmers to buy local food from. Soon after, Chris Krucker of ManoRun Organic Farm approached us about ordering his produce for our kitchen. Chris appeared at a moment of synchronicity—we had long wanted to provide a dining experience that would illustrate the journey of food from farm to restaurant. ManoRun would supply our kitchen with delicious locally grown, seasonal produce, and we and our staff would have the opportunity to dig in the dirt by working at the farm. What followed was a deep lesson in the differences between restaurants and farms, and farmers and chefs, and it was the inspiration for our first book, *Earth to Table: Seasonal Recipes from an Organic Farm*.

Earth to Table followed a year-long journey of food from Chris's farm to our restaurant tables at Ancaster Mill, and celebrated the glorious benefits of eating seasonally. For us it was a watershed moment. Much has happened since *Earth to Table* was published in 2009. Back then, farmers' markets were just beginning to wedge themselves

into urban spaces in towns and cities across the country. Today, throughout spring, summer, and autumn, you can find local farmers, both new and old generation, selling hormone- and antibiotic-free meat and free-range eggs alongside locally grown fruits and vegetables, fresh-baked goods, and artisanal honey in urban parking lots and disused spaces between buildings. All that delicious growth affected us in powerful ways and was the motivation behind long-held dreams.

As chefs tend to do during punishing restaurant hours, we fantasize about opening our own place: Jeff wanted to open a pizzeria; Bettina, a bakery. Push led to shove led to leap and—with some outside encouragement—Bread Bar was born. We were astonished at how quickly the restaurant became a popular hangout on the local dining and take-out scene. When we first opened, we needed a single 50-pound bag of flour a day to make pizza dough. Now we go through many, many more.

At first, we planned to offer counter service only, but the overwhelming demand for food made with "good ingredients that matter" led us to add a bar and more restaurant seating a year or so later, and the basement eventually became baker's central for all our operations. It wasn't long before we opened another Bread Bar restaurant, this time in Guelph, and as we write this there are plans for a third. Our restaurants embrace the earth-to-table philosophy that permeates our seasonal menus and our approach to food. Customers immediately welcomed our fresh, seasonal dishes and supported us as we experimented to find a balance between food that was familiar and comforting and a menu that changed with the weather.

One of the lessons we learned through our relationship with Chris Krucker and ManoRun Organic Farm is that we are not farmers. Just like the restaurant life, farming is gruelling work and not for the faint of heart or body. Nature can bless and damn you in the same year. Thankfully, there are more young farmers willing to dig deep and take on the challenge so that we can focus on cooking good food.

But one thing we noticed is that for many new farmers, the greatest barrier to living their dream is a lack of access to land. This challenge was one of the reasons we decided to purchase some farmland with our company Pearle Hospitality in 2010. There, in partnership with an amazing organization called Farm Start, we set up an organic "incubator farm," at the time one of only two in Canada. We set aside fifty acres to rent out to budding farmers who practise organic agriculture, and each farmer gets four years to make their efforts work as a complete business. Rowena Cruz, a computer animator who originally showed up at the Ancaster Mill's kitchen door selling her tomatoes, was one of those incubator farmers. Today, she is one of our field managers and probably the most successful farmer to come out of the Earth to Table farm. For Bread Bar, we currently plant six acres, on which Rowena is growing cucumbers, squash, lettuce greens, tomatoes, and much more for us. Every winter our chefs meet to pore over seed catalogues and plan for the spring planting.

Something else that became apparent was that through our connection with local farmers, we connected even more deeply with the community around Bread Bar. People came to us for coffee, business lunches, pizza runs, family dinners, and celebrations. Even the core contingent of recipe testers for this book hail from the neighbourhood. They are committed to our food and what it represents.

That community goodwill made us realize it was time to write another cookbook—one that celebrates how good food can enrich your life every day. We are a duo of food hedonists: Bettina nurtures the authentic connection with the community and delights customers with her delicious and thoughtful approach to baking. Jeff is always seeking and exploring fresh flavours to create new favourites. You'll find all that salt-and-pepper goodness in this book's recipes because there is no pretense when it comes to Bread Bar's motto, "Good ingredients matter."

According to Lenore Newman, author of *Speaking in Cod Tongues*, Canadian cuisine has several defining features: wild food, indigenous food, and seasonal food, with a focus on ingredients ahead of recipes. All these elements are in tangible evidence at Bread Bar. Bettina has foraged for garlic ramps for topping pizza and hauled a bumper crop of rhubarb from her backyard to the restaurant to use in pies and scones. Wild rice in a spicy lentil salad and rainbow trout cooked campfire style embrace the indigenous element. And the summer heat floods us with sweet tomatoes from local farmers for our Heirloom Tomato Salad (page 58), an homage to the seasonal along with many other fruits and vegetables.

The tricky thing about eating seasonally is that it's much harder to achieve in a four-season climate where the growing season is unpredictable. By the time spring's bounty starts to arrive at our doorstep, people are wearing shorts in anticipation of summer's heat and may not be interested in eating asparagus or ramps. August is one of those months where we simply can't keep up with the amount of fresh produce arriving daily at the kitchen, though we do our best to preserve as much as possible for use during the dreary days of winter.

Bread Bar excels at showcasing good ingredients in simple dishes that keep drawing customers back. For us, delicious, good food is the priority. And that begins with the choice of ingredients. When you read a menu, your cravings often guide your choice of meal, and often that means locking on to an ingredient that you know and love, whether that is beets or arugula, steak or chicken, vanilla or chocolate. And when that familiar ingredient is prepared and presented with creativity and thoughtfulness, it can become something new and exciting, familiar and fresh simultaneously. That is the essence of good food.

For us, ingredients are paramount, but not just the ones that ripen on vines or are hidden in the soil, or live in the fields and on farms. The ingredients of goodness, community, comfort, taste, and joy are interwoven in every dish that graces our tables. That sounds complicated, but it isn't. It's essentially what we all hope for when we sit down at a family meal. We encourage home cooks to visit the farmers' markets rather than the grocery store and not only rediscover where their food comes from but experience the fun of doing so. Above all, this book insists on experiencing the flavour of joy.

Good food is neither simple nor uncomplicated when you consider the chemistry of flavour and texture. But it can be simple if you take the time to savour it. Eating a meal isn't supposed to mimic speed-dating. In an era where mindfulness is marketed as an antidote to the "fear of missing out," the case for enjoying good food is not an opportunistic public relations gimmick. You will miss out on something good—and miss out on joy—if you treat a meal as immediate rocket fuel, ingredients as a medicine chest, and cooking as a chore.

This book explores familiar ingredients and dishes in a fresh way, and encourages you to respect the flavour inherent in good food. Enhance it, but don't overwhelm it. That's part of Bread Bar's secret to success, and what we want to share with you in this book. This is our version of seasonal, fresh, delicious food.

COMMUNITY

For some people, a community is simply a group of people who live in the same locale and share schools, libraries, shops, and restaurants. On a more intimate level, a community can be a gathering of like-minded individuals, such as people who share a community oven in a neighbourhood park or who participate in a book club or a local soccer league. For us, and all our staff at Bread Bar, a community is a group of people who work together to achieve a common goal. It is an idea that evokes similar feelings of comfort and connectivity. Community is a place where we can recharge in an atmosphere of acceptance.

Strong, healthy communities are supportive, encouraging, and engaging. They foster happiness and stability and improve our quality of life. Yet the most important quality of community is its elastic ability to shape its environment. Since Bread Bar opened, we have seen remarkable changes take place in our urban locations. New restaurants and coffee houses have moved in around us, new stores have opened, a local realtor moved into a nineteenth-century bank next to the dollhouse-like library, and a seasonal farmers' market has sprung up in an unused auto shop lot on the weekends. Our locale has become a destination— the best evidence of a thriving community.

We like to think that we've created a local restaurant community at the Bread Bar locations, something in which we take great pride. We offer a place for friends to gather for coffee in the morning, a family-friendly restaurant where at times we have more child customers than adult ones, and a bakery where customers buy pies and fresh loaves of bread for dinner at home. Our customers truly consider Bread Bar a gathering place for their community, and it's an extraordinary,

interdependent relationship. They tell us what they want to eat and drink, and they aren't shy about telling us if the music's too loud or the room is too hot. We listen to our customers and encourage their participation. Though there are times when we don't like what we hear, and it may take a moment for a bruised ego to heal (the music usually *is* too loud), we greatly value the interdependent relationship and work hard to maintain it.

We also encourage our staff to weigh in on all aspects of life at Bread Bar, and part of staff training includes nurturing the fluid community that passes through our doors. Greeting customers by name is just one example. That's easy when some people visit Bread Bar several times a day—we have customers who come in for coffee in the morning, then again a few hours later to grab some cookies for the children's lunches. We see them again at lunchtime, when they choose a slice of pizza at the counter, and then perhaps at dinner, when they bring in the whole family. Other customers may visit weekly or monthly, but over the course of several years, familiarity and friendship is the natural outcome.

The strength of our community bond was borne out when we began to write this cookbook. Translating restaurant recipes for the home kitchen can be a challenge. Measurements might be off, cooking times can vary, and ingredients aren't always easy to substitute when needed. We put a modest notice up on our front door asking whether anyone would be interested in helping us test the recipes for home use. The response was overwhelming. About eighty people from the community contacted us. To help us whittle down that number, we asked them each to submit a short essay explaining why they thought they would be a good tester. Many sent us truly inspiring stories about their relationship with food and cooking. Out of the numerous responses we received, we chose a small group of testers and assigned recipes randomly. They were given a list of questions to answer about the cooking process, and we were genuinely fascinated by how thoughtful their comments were. These individuals, strangers at first, became community partners, and have had a deep hand in shaping the recipes you find here.

When we opened the first Bread Bar in 2010, the community responded immediately and positively. Between our staff and customers, we have a space that enjoys the signature virtues of community: it is supportive, encouraging, inclusive—and joyous. For anyone who might wish to join the fun, the doors are always open.

GOOD INGREDIENTS MATTER

At Bread Bar we talk about authenticity often. For us, it's about being genuine. But we also agree that it's a powerful challenge to live authentically in a fast-paced world, and even more difficult to deliver an authentic dining experience. We are purists when it comes to food, and our desire to be genuine about this is the inspiration behind the words emblazoned on the dining room walls: "good ingredients matter." These three words govern everything we purchase, make, and take to our tables. Our decisions are deliberate, from our choice to focus on local craft breweries instead of big corporate beers, all the way down to using natural sweeteners instead of artificial ones for coffee. The concept even guides how we do business, from supporting other local businesses to fostering the relationship with our staff.

We are constantly exploring how to offer authenticity by focusing on our love of good food. As a result, customers trust our food as well as changes we make to the menu or the restaurant setting. When we switched to using a locally made condiment, some customers felt we'd given up the flavour of the imported version, but many more were happy with our decision. We count on customers to tell us when we miss the mark, which liberates us to be transparent and vulnerable, which in turn allows us to become more open, honest, and engaged with our customers. The free flow of trust means our customers both accept our fallibility and applaud our ability to recover from missteps. That same sense of trust encourages customers to bring in their friends and families to share the experience at both Bread Bar locations.

Customer support is key in our mission for authenticity, but just as important is staff support. We encourage all our staff to get involved and to share their ideas. In many cases, we have used their ideas and sing their names in recognition. A few years ago, for example, Cam Bell, one of our chefs, developed a keen interest in barbecue. The next week Jeff showed up with a beautiful offset smoker, so big it has to rest on a trailer. Now each summer we offer the best slow-and-low brisket and pork shoulder north of the border, thanks to Cam's genuine love of this style of cooking.

When our staff are engaged in and validated by their experience working at Bread Bar, they, too, feel good about what we are doing and are happy to be at work.

We are also extremely proud of the relationships we have built with our food producers and suppliers. It's important to us that the people we choose to do business with are people with whom we share the same core value of authenticity. We don't have a set list of national suppliers. Instead, we have a long list of local purveyors with whom we are on a first-name basis, like Bob the Shoot Boss, who grows and delivers our microgreens, and Perry, who brings us our flour, and Brian, our favourite wine rep, who gives a Christmas present every year to each location along with a handwritten card addressed with the names of every staff member. Many of these business relationships have turned into mutually supportive friendships, and some are even problem solvers. One summer we needed to find a hardy green to top our Farm Green Pizza. Back 40 Farm showed up with the perfect one, called Pomegranate Crunch, a lovely lettuce tinged with pink that highlighted the summer season.

Our core value of authenticity—that good ingredients matter—provides us with confidence in what we place on the table at Bread Bar and how it is served. But the drive to be genuine also pushes us beyond the front door and out into the community. We are particularly proud of our involvement with Restaurants for Change, a group that raises funds to support community food programs all across Canada. In our community, funds we raise for this group are delivered directly to a new community food centre. We also partner with programs such as Food4Kids, which strive to ensure that all kids have access to healthy food. If anyone can benefit most from an authentic relationship with food, it is kids.

As we have grown, Bread Bar has met with obstacles that challenge our core values, but because we are both hands-on with the daily operations, we are free to make changes when the need arises. We have discovered that being authentic is not an all-or-nothing proposition; authenticity requires flexibility and versatility. We have our moments that we like to call "wince time" when we look into the walk-in fridges and spots a few less than ideal ingredients. But those go to the top of the list to be removed from the restaurant. Always looking to improve, not being paralyzed by that task—we relish it. We never cease facing challenges; that nurtures our success.

NUTRITIONISM

If there is anything we want you to take away from this cookbook, it's that we love good food. At Bread Bar we celebrate what is best about food—real food, good food—and we want our passion and enjoyment to come through in these pages. But we also want to caution you not to get caught up in the ideology of "nutritionism." Our friend Michael Pollan argues that large food producers and their marketing machines have reduced the concept of food to simply its delivered (or not delivered) nutrients. For example, yogurt has suddenly become a provider of probiotics, eggs are Omega-3s, and olive oil is now cholesterol free! Our experience with the troubling trend of nutritionism is that our beloved bread has become the latest food villain via gluten. Certain foods are not ingredients or even food anymore; they have been reduced to the nutritional benefit they represent. Even quinoa, rice, icing sugar, and baking powder are now labelled "gluten-free" to entice and placate the gluten avoiders. How have we become consumers of nutrition as opposed to eaters of food?

Our earliest memory of *nutritionism* in action is margarine, a tale that neatly documents this perplexing turn of events in the food world. Manufacturers and marketers held the purported health benefits of margarine to be more important than the reality that margarine is a "food-like" substance.

Margarine is an oil-based product, with a butter-like texture and mouthfeel, and it was dyed yellow to resemble butter. When cold, margarine spreads more easily than butter does, which, along with its lower price, made it a favourite with consumers. As most of us know today, most margarines were made of hydrogenated oil containing unhealthy trans-fats. Some margarine manufacturers have now opted to use fewer or no trans-fats in their product—and have used this as yet another marketing gimmick. But the point is, the philosophy of nutritionism, allowed us to believe that margarine was a healthy alternative to butter, even though today we know that the health risks of margarine outweigh those of butter. Not to mention the amazing flavour and incredible versatility of butter within cuisine.

Michael Pollan introduced us to the concept of nutritionism with his 2007 *New York Times* article "Unhappy Meals," an essay that was the genesis for his bestselling book *In Defense of Food*. And it is Pollan's most widely

quoted recommendation from that book—"Eat food, not too much, mostly plants"—that has validated much of how we think about the food we serve at Bread Bar.

Nutritionism shows its contradictory face at our restaurants in the requests we get to change dishes to accommodate customers' dietary needs. We do the best we can, wherever possible, but sometimes the requests seem inconsistent where health needs are concerned. A customers might ask for a cheese-free pizza, but the white sauce on that pizza, made with butter and milk, passes muster.

As ever, flexibility has its place. As a baker, Bettina is never impressed with the taste or mouthfeel of gluten-free baked goods. Nevertheless, we offer plenty of gluten-free options, though we have yet to meet that gluten-free flour that perfectly replicates the texture and flavour of wheat flour. We use shortening in our pie dough, as we find it delivers the flakiest and most flavourful crust. We know shortening is a trans-fat, but the crust is a small part of the pie, given that our pies are chock full of healthy fruit and finished with an oatmeal-based crumble topping. These are the small concessions we make for the promise of good food. (You can find our Basic Pie Dough recipe on page 231. Try it with any fruit you like. We guarantee it will become your favourite pie.)

A firm commitment to cooking with the highest-quality, seasonal, fresh ingredients underlies everything we do at Bread Bar. We believe that if you start with thoughtful, hand-selected ingredients, cooking can be approached with a fresh attitude and a curiosity that will encourage you to dive into the recipes this book has to offer.

THE PROMISE OF GOOD FOOD

As chefs, we have both spent years in various upscale restaurant kitchens producing gourmet food that takes numerous people to execute. Once we had spent some time exploring culinary culture at the upscale level, we knew we needed to create Bread Bar to simplify the cooking and make good food available to our city. Bread Bar is much more casual than our previous service styles, but it centres on what we both believe to be the essential component of any meal: good food. And though we don't consider ourselves nutrition experts, we do know what makes great food.

Great food is obvious: it tastes delicious; it's fresh, genuine, and free of unnecessary additives; it has nutritional value and will do no harm if eaten in moderation. Good food has

everyday ingredients that you recognize. For instance, Bettina frequently makes banana bread with her daughter. The ingredient list is a short one: flour, brown sugar, eggs, overripe bananas, leavening, and sour cream. Jeff is inspired by the seasons to help him keep it simple at home. No tomatoes until summer. Only then does he make a great Heirloom Tomato Salad (page 58). Putting good food on the table, whether it's in our restaurant or in your own home, takes effort and mindfulness, but it is worth every bite.

The most delicious and nutritious food will come directly from the land, whether you grow it in your own backyard or buy it at a farmers' market. Growing your own can be surprisingly easy, and is supremely gratifying (though we're not suggesting everyone start their own homestead and boycott the local grocery store). You don't necessarily need a big garden. Lettuces, strawberries, and many tomatoes, for example, grow well in pots on a deck and in balcony planters. Pick one vegetable or fruit and see where that takes you. Select something you know you'll use (remember all those shallots you tossed in the compost?). Tomatoes can be a good place to start, and there are so many varieties to choose from. When Super Sweet 100s—a cherry tomato that can hold a hundred tomatoes or more on their stems—are at their peak, they are like candy, sweet and delicious. If you are not able to plant vegetables or fruits, then head to a farmers' market and support your local purveyors and food artisans. A farmers' market can be like a culinary school, with producers ready to answer all your food questions.

When it comes to grocery stores, focus on food that is as close to nature as possible. The perimeter of the grocery store—the produce section, butcher, seafood counter, and dairy bar—is where you'll find food, good food. Be wary when you enter those aisles lined with boxes and bottles and other food imposters that come in alluring packages. Be aware that packaging with a long list of chemicals or too many health claims are also red flags. These days we venture into the middle aisles only for coffee, tea, oils, vinegar, dried or canned legumes, dried pasta, and rice. (Oh, and potato chips when Jeff craves them!)

The recipes in this cookbook are based on these foundations. They've been tested rigorously by our Bread Bar community for home use, and written so that whatever your skill level is in the kitchen, you will have success. Do what you can, one step at a time, and applaud yourself for every step you take.

BREADS

CHAD ROBERTSON

TARTINE BAKERY, SAN FRANCISCO, CALIFORNIA

Sourdough bread and San Francisco have a long and deep history. Historically sourdough's fame began with Boudin Bakery, which opened in 1849, but the art of making sourdough bread was revived during the artisanal bread movement in the 1980s. Today numerous bakeries in the Bay Area, such as Acme Bakery, which opened in 1983, bake this beloved staple. Even when Jeff was going through cooking school in the late '90s, everyone knew that if you wanted to learn how to make sourdough bread you went to San Francisco. Then along came Chad Robertson, and the game changed. Chad Robertson's sourdough bread is the gold standard that we hold each and every loaf up to.

In 2002 Chad opened Tartine Bakery with his wife, Elisabeth Prueitt. He started to make bread with the basic tools he'd learned during his stints in various old-world bakeries in France and later in the U.S. And then he created a sourdough loaf of his own. Over a six-year period of trial and error, in a small and secluded space in Point Reyes, California, he developed a loaf with a firm, dark, and blistered crust and with an interior that was creamy, open, and delicious. When he was ready, he shared his secrets in his 2010 book, *Tartine Bread*.

Chad laid out the process step by step with accompanying photos to help the home baker. He described how the dough needed gentle mixing and a long fermentation, during which you gave the dough a series of "turns," or folds. He explained why he used more water than many recipes, and the importance of steam injection during the baking. While he was writing his book, he sent his recipes out to bread testers to make sure they would work in a home kitchen. At first he assumed that the testing process would be time consuming and overwhelming. But as the testers sent in their results, he soon realized they were making sourdough bread just as good as if it had come out of his own ovens.

Bettina discovered the magic of sourdough bread ten years earlier on a trip to San Francisco. She started baking it for our customers in 2001 at the Ancaster Mill with a starter she had cultivated. Bettina was reasonably assured she could figure it out on her own, but despite research, lots of reading, and Jeff's input, initial attempts were barely passible. Bettina took a few sourdough bread courses and heavy loaves became lighter, and less sour. Jeff seemed to like them, but Bettina knew something was not quite right.

Then a perfectly funny thing happened. Katrina, an inquisitive staff member who had helped us to open Bread Bar, asked to work in the kitchen as a baker. Bettina spent about a year teaching her about pastry and baking, and then Katrina made the decision to go to San Francisco with the promise she would be back. She studied at the famed San Francisco Baking Institute, learning about bread the old-school way, and then spent time working in several San Francisco bakeries, including Tartine. To our delight, she did return. Jeff stopped her at the back door and asked the big question.

"Can you make it?" "Can you make a Tartine-style bread?" With a knowing glance and big smile Katrina nodded her head—and became our head baker—and brought with her all the secrets of the elusive San Francisco sourdough bread.

Now we have our own sourdough loaf at Bread Bar in the fine tradition of Tartine bread. Our bakers work through the night so our sourdough loaves are available first thing in the morning. The dough goes through a long, cool fermentation to give the bread that characteristic taste that comes with natural fermentation. The main differences between the Tartine sourdough bread and ours are that we use Canadian flours, and of course the wild yeasts in the air are different. Other differences are subtle and reflect the environment the bread is made in and the bakers who add their own experience. Bread has many nuances, and Bettina can often tell which of our bakers has made the bread just by looking at it. We still make a regular bread whose dough goes through a long fermentation, but, of the two, the sourdough is the most prized. It sells out the quickest and is used the most by the kitchen. This is the result of a decade-long search for the perfect loaf of bread.

Chad Robertson is still challenging North American bread makers to make better bread. He is now trying to develop a loaf that can be enjoyed by people with gluten sensitivities, working with ancient flours and grains that have lower gluten levels. It's hero's work. We take inspiration from Chad. He keeps us curious about bread, and we share his enthusiasm in sharing the results.

STEELTOWN CRUSTY BREAD

MAKES 1 LOAF • REQUIRES TIME FOR PREP

"Can you make it?" That was the first question Jeff had for our head baker, Katrina Vandenberg, when she returned from studying bread making in California. The bread in question was a crusty, airy sourdough from Tartine Bakery in San Francisco, our favourite loaf of all time. Her answer was yes, delivered with a knowing, excited smile. High-fives and a big hug later, we knew we had just stepped it up another level.

We make naturally fermented sourdough loaves, which requires a major time commitment. Using instant yeast in this recipe makes things easier for the home baker. As your skill level and confidence increase, make your own Sourdough Starter (page 16) and use it in place of the instant dry yeast in this recipe.

At Bread Bar we use special bread-baking ovens with stone floors and steam injection. Steaming the loaves at the beginning of baking allows for a beautifully domed loaf and a glossy, caramelized crust. The traditional method of replicating this in a home oven was to use a clay pot with a lid, called a cloche. The steam is generated from the bread itself and is captured within the vessel. Many home cooks have enamelled cast-iron pots, so that's what we have used for this recipe. We use this bread for our Toast Four Ways (page 89), but the possibilities are limitless!

1. In a large bowl, combine the flour, yeast, and salt. Add the warm water and stir until blended. The dough will be shaggy and sticky. Cover the bowl with plastic wrap and let the dough rest at room temperature for 7 to 18 hours. The longer the dough ferments, the more distinctive characteristics there will be in the crust, crumb, and flavour.

2. To fold the dough, wet your hands and, with the dough still in the bowl, carefully pull the edge farthest from you up towards you and fold the dough in half once. Press or pinch the dough down to set a seam around the edges. Turn the bowl a quarter turn and fold the dough over the same way. Turn the bowl one more time and fold the dough over. Cover loosely with plastic wrap and let rest for about 30 minutes.

3. Fold the dough three times again, turning the bowl a quarter turn between folds. Allow the dough to stretch itself; you are just the guide. Do not tear the dough. If the dough tears, it has not rested long enough since that first folding. Cover the bowl loosely with plastic wrap and let the dough rest for 1 hour. Repeat step 3.

3 cups (750 mL) unbleached organic bread flour, more for dusting
¾ teaspoon (4 mL) instant dry yeast (or ¼ cup/60 mL Sourdough Starter, page 16)
1 tablespoon (15 mL) kosher salt
2 cups (500 mL) warm water

(RECIPE CONTINUES…)

4. Place a 4½- to 5½-quart (4.5 to 5.5 L) pot with a lid (preferably enamelled cast iron such as Le Creuset #24 or #26) in the oven and preheat the oven to 450°F (230°C).

5. When the oven is up to temperature, carefully remove the pot. Slide your hand under the dough, lift it from the bowl, and flip it over right into the pot. It may look like a mess, but that's okay. Shake the pot once or twice if the dough is unevenly distributed; it will straighten out more as it bakes. Cover, return to the oven, and bake for 30 minutes.

6. Remove the lid and bake for another 15 to 30 minutes, until the loaf is a dark nut brown. Remove from the pot and cool on a rack. The crust will begin to snap, crackle, and pop as it cools and contracts. Let the bread cool for at least 1 hour before slicing.

7. After a day, store the loaf in a resealable plastic bag for up to 2 days.

MAKE YOUR OWN SOURDOUGH STARTER

MAKES 2 CUPS (500 ML) STARTER • REQUIRES TIME FOR PREP

The first step in making a sourdough starter is to throw out your fear and earn some patience. You do not need a secret ritual, fermented grapes, or an heirloom recipe. It is as plain and simple as letting flour and water sit. In fact, you let it go sour, which sounds counterintuitive because we spend so much effort keeping our foods from going sour. In this case, let your starter go sour and then keep it that way and you are going to make delicious bread. We suggest using plastic or glass containers, as metal bowls may react to the acidic starter. Your starter will take about 5 days to get bubbling. It thrives in still air around 77°F (25°C). We suggest keeping your starter on top of your fridge or in a cupboard.

DAY 1: MAKE THE STARTER

1½ cups (375 mL) unbleached organic bread flour
½ cup (125 mL) organic whole wheat flour (we use Red Fife)
½ cup (125 mL) warm water

1. Combine the bread flour, whole wheat flour, and warm water in a medium plastic or glass container. Stir until a stiff dough is formed. Scrape down the sides and loosely cover the container with a clean kitchen towel. Place in a draft-free area at warm room temperature. Let it sit for 24 hours.

1. With each feeding, remove 1 cup (250 mL) of starter and discard. Add the bread flour, whole wheat flour, and warm water to the starter dough and stir until it becomes like a lump-free dough. Scrape down the sides and loosely cover the container with a clean kitchen towel. Place in a draft-free area at warm room temperature. Repeat this process every 24 hours.

2. Each day, take a look at your starter and note the changes. Are there bubbles? Are they large or small? Small bubbles will form at the beginning of fermentation, becoming larger towards the end. Is the starter increasing in volume? Is it starting to smell sour? Taste it: it should be starting to taste somewhat vinegary. If not, don't worry, it just needs more time. You will not notice many changes the first couple of days, but by Day 4 it should be obvious that things are happening.

3. When your starter has doubled in volume, is webbed with bubbles, and smells sour and pungent, it is ripe and ready to use to make bread. Whenever you use your starter, make sure to keep 1 cup (250 mL) to feed for the next time—keep the process rolling.

¾ cup (175 mL) unbleached organic bread flour
¼ cup (60 mL) whole wheat flour (we use Red Fife)
¼ cup (60 mL) warm water

FEEDING A STARTER (KEEPING IT ALIVE)

1. It takes daily care to keep your starter alive. Each day, preferably around the same time, "feed" your starter. Remove 1 cup (250 mL) of your starter, and discard the remainder. In a clean medium glass or plastic container, combine the reserved starter, the bread flour, whole wheat flour, and warm water. Cover with a clean kitchen towel and keep in a draft-free area at warm room temperature.

1 tablespoon (15 mL) starter
¾ cup (175 mL) unbleached organic bread flour
¼ cup (60 mL) whole wheat flour (we use Red Fife)
¼ cup (60 mL) warm water

WHITE PAN BREAD

MAKES 2 LOAVES • REQUIRES TIME FOR PREP

Every sandwich we serve at Bread Bar is made from bread that was baked in-house that morning.
We are very proud of this. At a time when restaurants serve frozen dinner rolls, we are champions of the bakers
who work when we are all asleep, the unsung heroes of our breakfast, lunch, and dinner.
This bread is best for sandwiches such as our Porchetta Sandwich (page 119).

6½ cups (1.625 L) unbleached organic
   bread flour
¼ cup (60 mL) sugar
2 tablespoons (30 mL) kosher salt
4 teaspoons (20 mL) instant dry yeast
2 cups (500 mL) warm water
¾ cup (175 mL) whole milk
4 tablespoons (60 mL) shortening

1. In the bowl of a stand mixer fitted with the dough hook, combine the flour, sugar, salt, and yeast. Add the warm water and milk, and stir on the lowest speed until blended; the dough will be shaggy and sticky. While stirring, add the shortening 1 tablespoon (15 mL) at a time. Knead on low speed for 10 minutes. If the dough sticks to the bowl, turn off the mixer and scrape down the sides. Remove the bowl from the mixer, cover with plastic wrap, and let the dough rise until doubled in size, 1 to 2 hours, depending on the warmth of your kitchen.

2. Grease two 9- x 5-inch (2 L) loaf pans. Tip the dough out onto a lightly floured work surface and press to gently deflate it. Cut the dough in half and gently fit each piece into a loaf pan. Cover the pans with plastic wrap and let the dough rise until it's just below the lip of the pan, about 1 hour, depending on the warmth of your kitchen.

3. While the dough rises, preheat the oven to 400°F (200°C).

4. Bake the loaves for 25 minutes, or until they sound hollow when tapped, the tops are brown, and the internal temperature reaches 200°F (100°C). Remove the loaves from the pans and let cool on racks.

5. After a day, store the loaves in resealable plastic bags for up to 2 days or freeze for 2 weeks.

HERITAGE MULTIGRAIN BREAD

MAKES 2 LOAVES • REQUIRES TIME FOR PREP

In our first cookbook, *Earth to Table: Seasonal Recipes from an Organic Farm*, we talked about how Bettina spent four years sourcing Red Fife wheat seeds, then planting them at ManoRun Farm, harvesting them, and grinding them for this bread. Thanks to the great efforts of Slow Food and many like-minded chefs, home bakers now have improved access to fantastic heritage varieties of grains and flours. This is the perfect sandwich bread, because of its soft, creamy texture, for recipes like the Avocado, Tomato, Chicken, and Bacon Sandwich (page 124).

1. In the bowl of a stand mixer fitted with the dough hook, combine the bread flour, whole wheat flour, cereal, salt, and yeast. Add the warm water, milk, and honey, and stir on the lowest speed until blended; the dough will be shaggy and sticky. Knead on low speed for 10 minutes. If the dough sticks to the bowl, turn off the mixer and scrape down the sides. Remove the bowl from the mixer, cover with plastic wrap, and let the dough rise until doubled in size, 1 to 2 hours, depending on the warmth of your kitchen.

2. Grease two 9- x 5-inch (2 L) loaf pans. Tip the dough out onto a lightly floured work surface and press gently to deflate it. Cut the dough in half and gently fit each piece into a loaf pan. Cover the pans with plastic wrap and let the dough rise until it's just below the lip of the pan, about 1 hour, depending on the warmth of your kitchen.

3. While the dough rises, preheat the oven to 400°F (200°C).

4. Bake the loaves for 25 minutes, or until they sound hollow when tapped, the tops are brown, and the internal temperature reaches 200°F (100°C). Remove the loaves from the pans and let cool on racks.

5. After a day, store the loaves in resealable plastic bags for up to 2 days or freeze for 2 weeks.

4½ cups (1.125 L) unbleached organic bread flour

3 cups (750 mL) whole wheat flour (we use Red Fife)

½ cup (125 mL) seven-grain cereal (we use Anson Mills)

2 tablespoons (30 mL) kosher salt

2 tablespoons (30 mL) instant dry yeast

3 cups (750 mL) warm water

½ cup (125 mL) whole milk

1 tablespoon (15 mL) liquid honey

ROSEMARY FOCACCIA

MAKES 1 LARGE FLAT LOAF • REQUIRES TIME FOR PREP

Crusted with rosemary and sea salt, this Italian flat bread is a versatile addition to our menu. We use it for crostini, with our Marinated Chickpea Sandwich with Romesco Sauce (page 121), or as garlic bread with soups and pastas.

---

4 cups (1 L) unbleached organic bread flour

1 tablespoon (15 mL) kosher salt

1½ teaspoons (7 mL) instant dry yeast

2 cups + 1 tablespoon (515 mL) warm water

2 tablespoons (30 mL) extra-virgin olive oil, divided

2 tablespoons (30 mL) chopped fresh rosemary

Flaky sea salt (we use Maldon)

1. In the bowl of a stand mixer fitted with the dough hook, combine the flour, kosher salt, and yeast. Add the warm water and 1 tablespoon (15 mL) of the olive oil, and stir on the lowest speed until blended; the dough will be shaggy and sticky. Knead on low speed for 10 minutes. If the dough sticks to the bowl, turn the mixer off and scrape down the sides. Remove the bowl from the mixer, cover with plastic wrap, and let the dough rise in the fridge for 24 hours. The dough should double in size. (This cool, slow rise is where the magic happens. The dough will be easier to stretch and the focaccia will have a crisper crust and more flavour.)

2. Preheat the oven to 400°F (200°C) and line a baking sheet with parchment paper.

3. Tip the dough out onto the baking sheet and shape it into a rough disc about 2 inches (5 cm) thick. Drizzle the remaining 1 tablespoon (15 mL) olive oil over the dough and press down with your fingertips to create divots all over the surface. Sprinkle with rosemary and sea salt. Let the dough rest for 30 minutes.

4. Bake until golden and crisp, about 30 minutes. Transfer the focaccia to a rack and let cool completely.

5. After a day, store the focaccia in a resealable plastic bag for up to 2 days or freeze for 2 weeks.

SOUPS

TO EVERY
SEASON

For most of history, eating seasonally was not a choice but a necessity, as there was no refrigeration and, later on, imported fruits and vegetables were limited and expensive. But imports of fresh fruits and vegetables have increased substantially, and today your neighbourhood grocery store is selling lemons, limes, asparagus, bananas, and tomatoes year-round, alongside produce that was rarely seen only a decade or so ago—hello, Meyer lemons and black kale!

The return to eating seasonally today might have begun as a trend, but it has evolved into a deliberate choice. And amazingly it's happening everywhere. In restaurants and home kitchens, more people are paying attention to when local fruits and vegetables are at their peak, knowing that seasonal produce will always deliver the most delicious and intense flavour, is usually affordable, and often serves up the most health benefits. At Bread Bar we serve fresh tomatoes only when they're at their best in the summer and early fall. We still buy tomatoes in other seasons, but cooked tomatoes are used for tomato confit in sandwiches and of course on our pizzas.

In celebration of the seasons, the menu at Bread Bar changes four times a year, on the first day of each season. The spring menu is the one we struggle with every year. Since we live in a cold climate, as a chef Jeff can say confidently that spring is always the most anticipated season of them all, despite summer and fall's bounty. That's because after enduring a cold, icy winter full of squash and hearty stews, spring rushes in with warm sunshine, gentle rain, and an appetite for asparagus, rhubarb, and tender young greens. However, where we live, when the first day of spring arrives in March, the ground is usually frozen solid. So, what to do?

In the past, we would change over the winter menu to the spring one in the middle of May, around the same time asparagus and rhubarb were ready to be picked. Unfortunately, that meant we had only about six weeks until we launched the summer menu. After some wrangling, we decided to launch the spring menu on the official first day of spring anyway, anticipating that customers would call us out. Local asparagus in March? Impossible. But we discovered that everyone is looking forward to winter's end, and our customers were more than happy with our decision. A long season of inclement weather and snow shovelling takes a toll on all of us, so a fresh new menu presented a little early was welcomed with open arms. Jeff calls this "pushing the seasons." We cheat for the benefit of us all.

Right on schedule the farmers begin arriving at our door. One of our favourites is Rowena Cruz. Jeff met her about seven years ago, at a local farmers' market. At the time, we would buy wonderful Asian greens from Rowena: beautiful baby bok choy, napa cabbage (Chinese cabbage), and pea shoots. We did this for many years, but then Jeff stopped going to the market and the relationship fizzled. Then, a year later, Rowena stopped in to Bread Bar one day, offering fat tomatoes, ten different varieties and colours, and our mind was blown. Now Rowena is one of our field managers at Earth to Table Farm! Serendipity.

If you have made the decision to eat seasonally but don't have the time or space to grow your own produce, the smart place to shop is at farmers' markets. Besides contributing to your local economy and meeting new like-minded people, the bountiful months during spring, summer, and fall—and winter if you are lucky to live in a warmer clime—present a terrific opportunity to talk with the producers about what fruits and vegetables will be popping up next. And if you know what is coming up, you'll have the time to find recipes—or create your own—that will make the best of the season's lineup. Experiment with a new veggie, or give your favourite dessert crisp a new twist by using heirloom apples. Your taste buds will thank you.

1. Preheat the oven to 350°F (180°C). Line a baking sheet with parchment paper.

2. Using a vegetable peeler, remove the skin from the butternut squash and discard. Cut the neck off the squash and set it aside. Cut the bulb in half and scoop out and discard the seeds. Cut the squash into 1-inch (2.5 cm) cubes. In a large bowl, toss the squash with 2 tablespoons (30 mL) of the canola oil and 10 sage leaves. Spread the squash on the prepared baking sheet and bake until fork-tender, about 30 minutes. Let cool. Discard the sage leaves.

3. Heat the remaining 3 tablespoons (45 mL) canola oil in a medium pot over high heat. Add the leeks, carrots, and onions, reduce the heat to medium, and cook, stirring often, for 10 minutes.

4. Reserve 1 cup (250 mL) of the cooked squash for garnish. Add the remaining squash, the garlic, and a pinch of salt to the leek mixture and cook gently for 3 minutes, stirring often and reducing the heat as necessary to keep the vegetables from sticking to the bottom of the pan. Add the chicken stock, bring to a simmer, and cook for 20 minutes. Add salt if the soup tastes flat. Let the soup cool slightly.

5. Working in batches, purée the soup in a high-speed blender until smooth. Return the soup to the pot, taste again and season with salt and pepper.

6. When ready to serve, gently reheat the soup. Heat a small skillet over medium heat. Add the butter and rotate the skillet over the heat to melt the butter evenly, scraping up any bits that settle to the bottom. As soon as the butter starts to show a light brown colour, add the remaining 8 sage leaves and swirl them in the butter for 30 seconds. Immediately pour the butter and sage leaves into a heatproof bowl to stop the cooking. Remove the sage leaves and drain on a paper towel; reserve the brown butter.

7. Serve the soup hot, garnished with the reserved squash, fried sage, a swirl of sour cream, and a drizzle of brown butter.

BUTTERNUT SQUASH SOUP

SERVES 4

This recipe is a slam dunk. If you want a happy family, feed them this soup. It is our go-to soup for any big event that we are catering in the fall. At the restaurant this soup goes on our menu as soon as it starts to get cold outside. It goes very well with the Squash and Apple Salad (page 53).

1 butternut squash (1 pound/450 g)
5 tablespoons (75 mL) canola oil, divided
18 fresh sage leaves, divided
1 cup (250 mL) thinly sliced leeks (white and light green part only)
½ cup (125 mL) peeled carrots cut into ¼-inch (5 mm) rounds
1 small white onion, thinly sliced
6 cloves garlic, minced
6 cups (1.5 L) chicken stock
Kosher salt and freshly ground pepper
4 tablespoons (60 mL) unsalted butter
2 tablespoons (30 mL) sour cream, for garnish

CORN AND POBLANO SOUP

This recipe is a spiced-up version of the corn soup in Jeff's worn notebook from when he was working in the kitchen at Chez Panisse. This is perfect soup to enjoy in July and August, when corn is in peak season. It goes well with the Heirloom Tomato Salad (page 58).

---

5 ears corn

8 cups (2 L) chicken stock

2 tablespoons (30 mL) unsalted butter

1 yellow onion, chopped

2 cloves garlic, minced

1 green poblano chili, seeded and chopped

2 Yukon Gold potatoes, peeled and cut into ½-inch (1 cm) cubes

1 tablespoon (15 mL) unseasoned rice vinegar

Kosher salt and freshly ground pepper

1 teaspoon (5 mL) cayenne pepper, for garnish (optional)

Fresh basil leaves, for garnish (optional)

1. Clean the corn of its husks and silks. Using a sharp knife, cut the kernels from the cobs and set aside. Place the stripped corn cobs in a large pot and add the chicken stock. Bring to a simmer and cook for 15 minutes. Remove and discard the cobs.

2. Melt the butter in a medium pot over high heat. Add the onion, garlic, poblano chili, and potatoes; cook, stirring occasionally, until the onions are translucent and tender, about 10 minutes.

3. Stir in the corn kernels and rice vinegar. Add the chicken stock, reduce the heat to medium, and simmer until the potatoes are fork-tender, about 20 minutes.

4. Season with salt and pepper. Serve garnished with cayenne and basil leaves, if using.

TUSCAN KALE AND BREAD SOUP

SERVES 4 TO 6 · REQUIRES TIME FOR PREP

The best Italian soups are chock full of vegetables, garlic, lemon, and cheese, making this soup eat like a meal. It pairs well with our Rosemary Focaccia (page 22) and is a hearty appetizer served before Braised Chicken Thighs with Green Olives and Pappardelle (page 168). If you have never cooked with real Parmigiano-Reggiano (the king of cheese) this soup is a great place to start. This soup improves if made a day ahead.

1. Heat the olive oil in a large pot over high heat. Add the celery, carrots, and onion; cook, stirring occasionally, until the onions are translucent and tender, about 10 minutes.

2. Reduce the heat to medium-high. Add the bay leaf, garlic, sage, rosemary, and salt. Cook for another 5 minutes.

3. Stir in the kale and tomatoes and cook for another 5 minutes. The aromas should be filling your kitchen. Add the chicken stock and simmer for 30 minutes.

4. Add the beans and chili flakes. Season with salt and pepper. Simmer for 10 minutes.

5. Add the bread cubes, stir well, and simmer for another 5 minutes. The bread will absorb the soup, which should be quite thick. Remove the bay leaf and stir in the lemon zest and juice. Serve with a generous amount of cheese over top.

¼ cup (60 mL) extra-virgin olive oil

3 stalks celery, diced

2 medium carrots, peeled and diced

1 medium white onion, diced

1 bay leaf

6 cloves garlic, minced

1 teaspoon (5 mL) minced fresh sage

¼ teaspoon (1 mL) minced fresh rosemary

2 teaspoons (10 mL) kosher salt

1 large bunch Tuscan black kale (about 1 pound/450 g), stemmed and chopped

1 can (14 ounces/398 mL) tomatoes, drained and chopped (or 3 fresh tomatoes)

4 cups (1 L) chicken stock

1 can (15 ounces/425 g) white navy beans, drained and rinsed

1 teaspoon (5 mL) red chili flakes

Freshly ground pepper

3 slices day-old Rosemary Focaccia (page 22 or store-bought), crust removed, cubed

Grated zest and juice of 1 lemon

Freshly grated Parmigiano-Reggiano cheese, for garnish

IRISH STEW

The key to any stew (or braise) is to pay attention to the first step, searing the meat. This is when you develop complex flavours on the meat, in the form of a deep caramel crust. The payoff is a rich, luscious stew. This stew is hearty enough to serve with just a salad. Our Heirloom Beet Salad with Salted Pumpkin Seeds and Feta (page 57) goes particularly well.

4½ pounds (2 kg) lamb shoulder chops, 1 inch (2.5 cm) thick
4 tablespoons (60 mL) vegetable oil, divided
1 medium onion, diced
¼ cup (60 mL) all-purpose flour
4 cups (1 L) water or chicken stock
1 teaspoon (5 mL) chopped fresh thyme
Kosher salt and freshly ground pepper
1½ teaspoons (7 mL) tomato paste
2 pounds (900 g) potatoes, peeled and cut into 1-inch (2.5 cm) pieces
1 pound (450 g) carrots, peeled and diced slightly smaller than the potatoes
¼ cup (60 mL) minced fresh flat-leaf parsley, for garnish

1. Preheat the oven to 300°F (150°C).

2. Cut the lamb from the bones, discarding the bones, and then cut the meat into 1½-inch (4 cm) pieces.

3. Heat 2 tablespoons (30 mL) of the vegetable oil in a Dutch oven over medium-high heat. Add enough of the lamb that the individual pieces are close together but not touching. Cook, without moving the lamb, until well browned on the bottom, 2 to 3 minutes. Using tongs, turn the lamb pieces and continue to cook until all sides are well browned. This will take about 15 minutes. The colour on the meat and the brown bits in the bottom of the pan will melt into the stew and provide great flavour. Set the seared lamb aside and repeat with the rest of the lamb, adding the remaining 2 tablespoons (30 mL) oil as needed. Set all the lamb aside when done.

4. Reduce the heat to medium, add the onion, and cook, stirring occasionally, until the onions are translucent and tender, about 10 minutes. Sprinkle with the flour and stir so the onions are evenly coated, scraping any remaining brown bits from the bottom of the pan.

5. Add the water, thyme, and a pinch of salt. Stir vigorously to break up any lumps of flour that may have formed. Add the tomato paste and the lamb with any accumulated juices. Return to a simmer, cover, and transfer to the oven. Cook for 1 hour.

6. Remove the pot from the oven and spread the potatoes and carrots on top of the lamb. Cover, return the pot to the oven, and cook until the lamb is tender, about 1 hour. Stir the stew gently and season with salt and pepper. Serve garnished with parsley.

CURRIED LENTIL SOUP WITH COCONUT YOGURT

SERVES 4 TO 6

This fantastically simple soup, puréed or not, is always a hit at Bread Bar. We all know that lentils are packed full of protein and fibre, but the earthiness of lentils and the tang of coconut yogurt is a combination we love. We serve this hearty soup with our Lamb Burger (page 116) or a Kale Caesar Salad (page 62).

---

1 tablespoon (15 mL) unsalted butter
3 tablespoons (45 mL) olive oil
1 medium onion, thinly sliced
2 medium carrots, peeled and grated
1 cup (250 mL) red lentils
5 cups (1.25 L) water or chicken stock
1 teaspoon (5 mL) minced fresh ginger
1 whole small hot chili (serrano, jalapeño, or habanero)
2 teaspoons (10 mL) ground coriander
1¼ teaspoons (6 mL) ground cumin
½ teaspoon (2 mL) turmeric
¼ teaspoon (1 mL) cayenne pepper
Kosher salt and freshly ground pepper

Coconut Yogurt
2 tablespoons (30 mL) plain full-fat yogurt
2 tablespoons (30 mL) coconut cream
2 tablespoons (30 mL) minced fresh cilantro

1. Melt the butter with the olive oil in a medium pot over medium-high heat. Reduce the heat to medium, add the onion, and cook, stirring occasionally, until the onions are translucent and tender, about 10 minutes.

2. Add the carrots, lentils, water, ginger, chili, coriander, cumin, turmeric, and cayenne; stir well. Bring to a boil, then reduce heat to a simmer, cover tightly, and simmer for 20 minutes or until the carrots are fork-tender. Taste and season with salt and pepper. Remove the chili pepper and discard.

3. To make the Coconut Yogurt, in a small bowl, stir together the yogurt, coconut cream, and cilantro.

4. Divide the soup among bowls and garnish with Coconut Yogurt.

CAULIFLOWER SOUP

SERVES 4

This simple yet rewarding soup is inspired by one of the best restaurants in the world, Chez Panisse, in Berkeley, California. This restaurant instilled in Jeff the idea that "good ingredients matter." This soup is an excellent accompaniment to our Grilled Lamb Chops (page 180).

1. Heat the olive oil in a medium pot over medium-high heat. Reduce the heat to medium, add the onion, and cook, stirring occasionally, until the onions are translucent and tender, about 10 minutes.

2. Add the cauliflower, chicken stock, and salt to taste. Return to a simmer. Then, reduce the heat to low, cover, and simmer for 20 minutes, or until the cauliflower is fork-tender.

3. Remove from the heat and cool slightly. Working in batches, purée the soup in a high-speed blender until smooth and creamy. We like to leave some of the soup chunky. Return the soup to the pot and season with salt and pepper.

4. Serve hot, garnished with parsley, a drizzle of mustard oil, and mustard to taste.

3 tablespoons (45 mL) olive oil
1 medium white onion, thinly sliced
2 pounds (900 g) cauliflower (about 1 large head), cored and broken into florets
5 cups (1.25 L) chicken stock
Salt and freshly ground pepper

Garnishes
2 tablespoons (30 mL) minced fresh flat-leaf parsley
2 tablespoons (30 mL) mustard oil or extra-virgin olive oil
1 tablespoon (15 mL) grainy mustard

TOMATO SOUP WITH FRIED CHICKPEAS

SERVES 4 TO 6

A lot of us grew up eating tomato soup the perfect way: served with saltine crackers and a grilled cheese sandwich. But adding fried chickpeas takes this classic soup to a new and modern level. We don't have a grilled cheese sandwich in our cookbook, but we do have Mac and Cheese (page 189)!

1. Heat the olive oil in a large pot over medium heat. Add the onion, celery, garlic, and chili flakes and cook, stirring occasionally, until the onions are translucent and tender, about 10 minutes.

2. Add the saffron (if using), tomatoes, and water. Reduce the heat to low and simmer, uncovered, for 20 minutes, stirring occasionally. Stir in the basil, then remove from the heat and let the soup cool for about 5 minutes.

3. Working in batches, purée the soup in a high-speed blender until smooth. Return the soup to the pot and season with salt and pepper. At this point you can make it nice and spicy with more chili flakes, if desired.

4. To make the Fried Chickpeas, heat the olive oil in a medium skillet over high heat. Add the chickpeas carefully, as they will spit and spatter. The chickpeas should be in one layer so each one is in contact with the pan. Fry for 3 minutes, swirling the pan occasionally. Add the garlic and cook for another 2 minutes, being careful not to let the garlic burn. A bit of browning on the chickpeas is okay. Drain the chickpeas, discarding the oil.

5. In a small bowl, season the Fried Chickpeas with salt and pepper, toss with the paprika and basil. (The Fried Chickpeas keep, covered at room temperature, for a few days.)

6. Serve the soup hot, garnished with the Fried Chickpeas.

2 tablespoons (30 mL) olive oil
1 medium onion, chopped
1 stalk celery, diced
3 cloves garlic, minced
1 teaspoon (5 mL) red chili flakes
Pinch of saffron threads (optional)
2 cans (28 ounces/796 mL each) crushed tomatoes
1½ cups (375 mL) water
¼ cup (60 mL) tightly packed fresh basil leaves
Kosher salt and freshly ground pepper

Fried Chickpeas
½ cup (125 mL) olive oil
1 cup (250 mL) canned chickpeas, rinsed and dried well
1 clove garlic, minced
Kosher salt and freshly ground pepper
1 teaspoon (5 mL) sweet paprika
1 tablespoon (15 mL) chopped fresh basil

WHITE GAZPACHO

SERVES 4 TO 6

This chilled gazpacho will take you directly to the hills of Spain on a hot summer day. White gazpacho has a truly special flavour, and it's ideal for entertaining because you make it ahead and just keep it in the fridge until you need it. We like to serve this soup with toasted Steeltown Crusty Bread (page 15) and our Pear and Prosciutto Sandwich (page 131).

2 pounds (900 g) green grapes
1 small cucumber, peeled, seeded, and
   chopped
2 green onions, chopped
2 slices day-old white bread, torn into
   small pieces
½ cup (125 mL) plain full-fat yogurt
¼ cup (60 mL) blanched almonds, toasted
¼ cup (60 mL) unseasoned rice vinegar
¼ cup (60 mL) buttermilk
2 tablespoons (30 mL) extra-virgin olive oil
1 tablespoon (15 mL) minced fresh dill
Pinch of cayenne pepper
Kosher salt and freshly ground pepper

Garnishes
Sliced green grapes
Extra-virgin olive oil
Minced fresh chives (optional)

1. In a medium bowl, combine the grapes, cucumber, green onions, bread, yogurt, almonds, rice vinegar, buttermilk, and olive oil. Stir once or twice, just to mix. Working in batches if necessary, purée the mixture in a high-speed blender until smooth. Transfer the soup to a large pitcher.

2. Stir in the dill and cayenne, then season with salt and pepper. Cover and refrigerate until cold. If you chill the soup overnight, whisk well before serving, as it may have separated.

3. Serve garnished with sliced grapes, a drizzle of olive oil, and chives, if using.

WATERMELON GAZPACHO

SERVES 4 TO 6 · REQUIRES TIME FOR PREP

This soup is bright, refreshing, and quintessentially summer. When we cater events in the summer, we often serve this soup as a passed appetizer in little shot glasses. But it's equally delicious served in bowls for lunch or as an appetizer at a summer dinner party. It goes well with our Roast Chicken with Watermelon and Pecan Salad (page 167).

1. Coarsely chop half the watermelon, half the cucumber, and half the green pepper. In a large bowl, combine the chopped watermelon, cucumber, green pepper, and onion. Toss lightly to mix. Add the garlic, chili, salt, and cayenne; mix well. Set aside.

2. Chop the remaining watermelon, cucumber, and green pepper into ¼-inch (5 mm) pieces. Place in a medium bowl and toss well so the flavours mingle. Add the olive oil and torn bread; mix well. Cover and refrigerate until cold, about 1 hour.

3. Working in batches if necessary, purée the chilled mixture in a high-speed blender until smooth. Transfer to a large pitcher and add the reserved vegetable mixture, the basil, sherry vinegar, and pepper to taste. Chill the soup for at least 2 hours to combine flavours. Serve chilled.

3 pounds (1.35 kg) watermelon (about 1 large watermelon), peeled
1 small cucumber, cut in half lengthwise and seeded
1 green bell pepper, cut in half and seeded
1 small red onion, chopped
2 cloves garlic, minced
1 small hot chili, stem removed, chopped (serrano, jalapeño, or habanero)
1½ teaspoons (7 mL) kosher salt
1 teaspoon (5 mL) cayenne pepper
½ cup (125 mL) extra-virgin olive oil
1 slice white bread, crust removed, torn into pieces
2 tablespoons (30 mL) minced fresh basil
2 tablespoons (30 mL) sherry vinegar
Freshly ground pepper

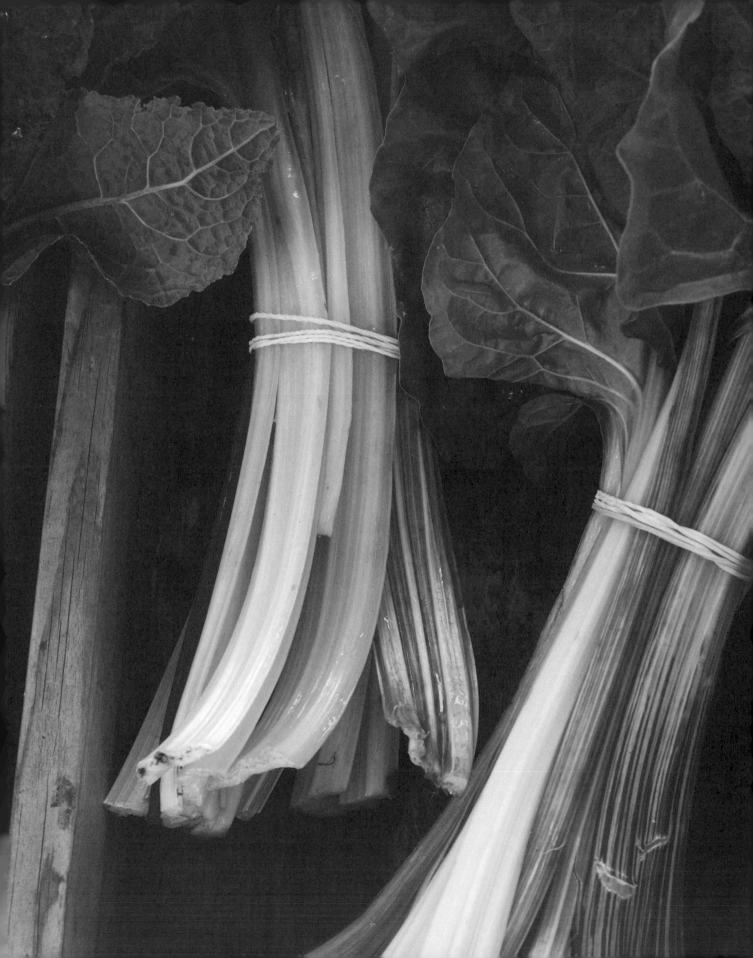

SALADS

DIGGING IN
THE DIRT

Bettina is not a particularly good gardener, but she really wants to be! Years ago, she planted an apple tree, thinking she could easily grow her own apples. She didn't know that another apple tree had to be within a certain distance so they could pollinate each other. Alas, the apple tree died from lack of lovin'. From then on, Bettina's gardening efforts have been a thrilling journey of trial and error. She has a great respect for farmers who grow produce as a profession.

Bettina now grows cucumbers, pie pumpkins, cherry tomatoes, beefsteak tomatoes, yellow grape tomatoes, popping corn, sweet corn, strawberries, white onions, and green onions, all with varying degrees of success. The snap peas didn't even germinate. And her sunflowers, though they grew and turned to follow the sun initially, at some point bowed their heads as if to say thanks for trying, but we're done. She did have huge success with jack-o'-lantern pumpkins one year, and they all graced her front porch proudly during Halloween. Today her most

successful garden plants—rhubarb, tomatoes, raspberries, and cucumbers—bring new life to the backyard every year. Some of the cucumbers make it into the Pimm's Cup Cocktail we serve at Bread Bar, and each bumper crop of rhubarb finds its way into our scones, pies, and smash-in ice cream.

Gardening requires patience and dedication. Patience is a skill that cooks like us must learn. But for those who have taken up the challenge of gardening find it immensely satisfying and enjoy a huge sense of accomplishment year in and year out. The ability to cultivate even a select few fruits or vegetables for use in home-cooked meals is gratifying and plays an important part in our well-being. Many people who garden appreciate the physical activity that comes from being outdoors and digging in the dirt. Others enjoy the solitude, the meditative experience. If you are growing vegetables or fruit in your yard or in some containers on your deck or balcony, you've brought yourself as close as possible to knowing where your food comes from. And truly fresh produce is always more nourishing and deeply satisfying.

Jeff has always believed that even simple gardening should be a mandatory activity for anyone with young children. There is no better way to teach the principles of health and good nutrition than showing kids what real food looks like in a garden. Each year Jeff invites school field trips to our Earth to Table farm. What the kids learn on our farm is that gardening is a physical act and digging in the dirt is the best way to know where your food comes from. Digging in the dirt shows us in real time what comes up from the ground in May or what can be harvested in October. And that nothing you can buy in the grocery store inspires the kind of pride and enjoyment that comes along with food you pick with your own hands. When kids see where food comes from, they gain a richer appreciation for it as well as a healthier relationship with it. Junk food suddenly becomes "junk." The kids immediately realize the difference between fast food and real, wholesome whole food.

As Bettina's experience has proven, if you are willing to relax and go with the flow, gardening doesn't need to be challenging, expensive, or complicated, even if you are living in an apartment or have no proverbial green thumb. Local nursery staff are often happy to help set you up with a pot, seeds, and soil. Herbs are a wonderful gateway to gardening success, especially when you start with such hardy plants as mint (which can take over your garden if not corralled), parsley, or sage. Before long you'll find yourself graduating to some of the more advanced crops, such as tomatoes, beans, and salad greens, as your space allows. And if space doesn't allow, then strawberries and some varieties of cherry tomato love to grow in hanging baskets. Remember to only plant the vegetables you use frequently, otherwise they will go to waste. The tricks to keeping your plants healthy and thriving are full sun, mindful watering, and rich soil. It doesn't have to be a time-consuming job, but fruits and vegetables are living species and need us to love them and take care of them.

ARUGULA AND FENNEL SALAD

SERVES 4

This simple yet refreshing salad has been on our menu since day one. It is so popular that we will never be able to take it off the menu. We did once, but we had a change of heart when we realized how much people loved it and how easily we could satisfy their craving.

1. Trim the stems off the fennel bulb and peel off any blemished outer layers with your fingers. Cut the fennel bulb in half from top to bottom and cut out the core of each half. Slice the fennel crosswise as thinly as you can, or shave it with a mandoline.

2. In a large salad bowl, combine the fennel, arugula, and House Vinaigrette. Season with salt and pepper and toss together.

3. Serve garnished with Parmesan, lemon zest, sunflower seeds, and a drizzle of Buttermilk Dressing.

1 medium fennel bulb
6 cups (1.5 L) tightly packed baby arugula (we prefer spicy wild arugula)
⅓ cup (75 mL) House Vinaigrette (page 244)
Kosher salt and freshly ground pepper

Toppings
2 ounces (55 g) Parmesan cheese, shaved with a vegetable peeler
1 tablespoon (15 mL) grated lemon zest
¼ cup (60 mL) raw sunflower seeds
2 tablespoons (30 mL) Buttermilk Dressing (page 243)

APPLE AND WALNUT SALAD

Farmers' markets across the country have contributed to the revival of many heirloom varieties of apples, and suddenly there is an amazing array to choose from. At our farm we have planted 15 varieties of eating and cider apples like Braeburn, Pink Lady, and Snow Apple. This salad combines the tart apple crunch with bitter radicchio, rich Brie cheese, and the sweet crunch of walnuts. It goes well with the Roasted Mushroom Pizza (page 150) or Ling Cod with Braised Cabbage and Apple (page 195).

3 Belgian endives, separated into leaves

1 head blond frisée lettuce, separated into leaves

1 head radicchio, leaves torn from ribs and thinly sliced

1 bunch watercress, trimmed

1 cup (250 mL) chopped walnuts

¼ cup (60 mL) dried cranberries

2 medium Empire or Northern Spy apples, cored and cut into thin wedges

3 tablespoons (45 mL) olive oil

2 tablespoons (30 mL) all-purpose flour

4 ounces (115 g) Brie, cut into eight ½-inch (1 cm) slices

⅓ cup (75 mL) House Vinaigrette (page 244)

Kosher salt and freshly ground pepper

1. In a large salad bowl, combine the endives, frisée, radicchio, watercress, walnuts, cranberries, and apples; toss gently to combine.

2. Heat the olive oil in a medium skillet over medium heat. Place the flour on a plate and firmly press both sides of the Brie slices in the flour until well coated. Shake off excess flour.

3. Reduce the heat to medium-low and carefully add the Brie slices. Cook for 1 minute on each side. Remove the Brie from the pan and drain on paper towel.

4. Add the House Vinaigrette to the salad, toss well, and season with salt and pepper. Divide the salad among plates and top each serving with a slice of fried Brie.

SQUASH AND APPLE SALAD

SERVES 4 TO 6

Each season we change some salads on our menu to reflect the current season's bounty. This is a favourite autumn salad at Bread Bar. Our customers love the contrast between the tang of the apples and richness of the squash. It goes well with our Cheese Burger (page 111) or the Butternut Squash Soup (page 29).

1. Preheat the oven to 350°F (180°C). Line a baking sheet with parchment paper.

2. Using a vegetable peeler, remove the skin from the butternut squash and discard. Cut the neck off the squash and set it aside. Cut the bulb in half and scoop out and discard the seeds. Cut the squash into 1-inch (2.5 cm) cubes.

3. In a large bowl, stir together the olive oil, sugar, cinnamon, cayenne, salt, and pepper. Add the squash and 3 of the apple halves. Toss well to coat with the spiced oil. Spread on the prepared baking sheet and bake until fork-tender, about 30 minutes. The apples may be done earlier, so be sure to remove them when fork-tender and set aside. Let the apples and squash cool completely.

4. Chop the cooled apples into bite-size pieces. In a large salad bowl, combine the apples and squash.

5. Thinly slice the remaining apple half and add to the salad. Add the watercress and House Vinaigrette and toss gently to combine. Season with salt and pepper. Serve garnished with Parmesan shavings and Crispy Quinoa.

1 large butternut squash
3 tablespoons (45 mL) olive oil
2 teaspoons (10 mL) sugar
¾ teaspoon (4 mL) cinnamon
⅛ teaspoon (0.5 mL) cayenne pepper
Kosher salt and freshly ground pepper
2 baking apples (Braeburn or Pink Lady), peeled, cored, and cut in half, divided
4 cups (1 L) watercress, trimmed
3 tablespoons (45 mL) House Vinaigrette (page 244)

Garnishes
3 ounces (85 g) Parmesan cheese, shaved with a vegetable peeler
2 tablespoons (30 mL) Crispy Quinoa (page 252)

SHAVED FENNEL AND CRAB SALAD

SERVES 4 TO 6

Fennel is one of our favourite vegetables. Crispy and tart with an amazing crunch, it pairs very well with seafood. If you are hosting a fancy brunch or dinner, king crab is the way to go, but this salad is also delicious made with smoked salmon, grilled trout, or poached shrimp instead of crabmeat.

---

6 tablespoons (90 mL) extra-virgin olive oil

4 teaspoons (20 mL) freshly squeezed lemon juice

2 teaspoons (10 mL) unseasoned rice vinegar

¾ teaspoon (4 mL) kosher salt

8 ounces (225 g) king crabmeat, picked over

Freshly ground pepper

1 medium fennel bulb

2 oranges (we use blood oranges when available)

4 radishes, thinly sliced

5 fresh basil leaves

4 fresh mint leaves

½ cup (125 mL) black olives, pitted, rinsed, and chopped

1. In a medium bowl, combine the olive oil, lemon juice, rice vinegar, and salt; whisk until well combined. Fold in the crabmeat and season with a few grinds of pepper. Set aside.

2. Trim the stems off the fennel bulb and peel off any blemished outer layers with your fingers. Cut the fennel bulb in half from top to bottom and cut out the core of each half. Slice the fennel crosswise as thinly as you can, or shave it with a mandoline. Set aside.

3. Slice the top and bottom off each orange. Place each orange, cut side down, on a cutting board. With a sharp knife, cut away the peel and pith, using downward motions to maintain the curvature of the fruit. Slice out the orange segments, leaving the membranes behind (or slice the peeled orange into rounds).

4. Scatter the shaved fennel, orange segments, radish slices, basil, mint, and olives over a platter. The result should be a playful mosaic effect. Evenly distribute the crabmeat over the salad, then spoon over the remaining dressing. Sprinkle lightly with salt and pepper and serve.

HEIRLOOM BEET SALAD WITH SALTED PUMPKIN SEEDS AND FETA

SERVES 4 • REQUIRES TIME FOR PREP

Roasting beets, rather than boiling them, keeps in the colour and all the flavour. It's the only way we cook beets at Bread Bar. Sherry vinegar gives these beets a tang that is just short of pickling. Using different-coloured beets in this dish makes for a visually stunning presentation. Look for different types, such as golden beets or Chioggia beets, and dress them separately so the dark red ones don't bleed their juices onto the lighter ones. You will have extra pumpkin seeds, which is a good thing, as they make a great snack. This salad goes well with our Mushroom Tarts with Taleggio Cheese (page 100).

1. Preheat the oven to 400°F (200°C).

2. To make the Beet Salad, cut the greens off the beets and discard, leaving about ½ inch (1 cm) of stem. Scrub the beets, pat dry, and toss with 2 tablespoons (30 mL) of the olive oil and the salt. Place the beets in a large roasting pan with ¼ cup (60 mL) water. Cover tightly with foil and roast until tender when pierced with a knife, about 40 minutes. Roasting time will depend on the size and type of beet, so it's best to check them earlier. Remove foil and let the beets cool. When cool enough to handle, peel the beets, then slice into wedges. Set aside.

3. While the beets are roasting, make the Salted Pumpkin Seeds. In a large cast-iron skillet over medium heat, toast the pumpkin seeds, stirring constantly, until puffed and slightly brown, about 10 minutes. Drizzle with olive oil, sprinkle with salt, and stir to coat. Remove from the heat. Serve warm or at room temperature. (The pumpkin seeds can be stored in an airtight container for up to 3 days.)

4. In a medium bowl, whisk in the remaining ½ cup (125 mL) olive oil, sherry vinegar, and shallot. Add the beets and stir well. Marinate for at least 2 hours or refrigerate for up to 12 hours. Drain the beets and discard the marinade.

5. In a medium serving bowl, combine the beets with the watercress and House Vinaigrette. Toss gently to mix. Garnish with ¼ cup (60 mL) Salted Pumpkin Seeds and the feta. Season with salt and pepper and serve.

Beet Salad

4 pounds (1.8 kg) beets, mixed colours
½ cup (125 mL) + 2 tablespoons (30 mL)
   extra-virgin olive oil, divided
½ teaspoon (2 mL) kosher salt
6 tablespoons (90 mL) sherry vinegar
1 shallot, thinly sliced

**Salted Pumpkin Seeds
(makes 1½ cups/375 mL)**

1½ cups (375 mL) raw pumpkin seeds
1 teaspoon (5 mL) extra-virgin olive oil
¼ teaspoon (1 mL) kosher salt

For Serving

4 cups (1 L) packed watercress leaves
¼ cup (60 mL) House Vinaigrette
   (page 244)
4 ounces (115 g) feta cheese, crumbled
Kosher salt and freshly ground pepper

HEIRLOOM TOMATO SALAD

SERVES 4 TO 6

Our approach to a good tomato salad is to keep it simple. Buying perfectly ripe tomatoes is by far the most important part of this recipe. Sweet, heavy-in-the-hand ripe summer tomatoes, salt, and extra-virgin olive oil are all you really need, but cucumber and mint add brightness, and good Greek feta cheese makes everything shine. This salad goes well with our classic Margherita Pizza (page 140).

2 pounds (900 g) ripe heirloom tomatoes, assorted colours
½ pound (225 g) heirloom cherry tomatoes, assorted colours
1 small cucumber, thinly sliced into rounds
2 cups (500 mL) packed baby arugula
¼ cup (60 mL) crumbled Greek feta cheese
¼ cup (60 mL) chopped fresh mint
Kosher salt and freshly ground pepper
⅓ cup (75 mL) extra-virgin olive oil

1. Wash, core, and slice the tomatoes into different shapes and wedges. Cut the cherry tomatoes in half. Arrange all the tomatoes on a platter.

2. Scatter the cucumber, arugula, feta, and mint over the tomatoes. The result should be a playful mosaic effect. Season with salt and pepper. Let sit for 10 minutes to draw out the juices.

3. Drizzle with the olive oil and serve.

CHOPPED SALAD

Salami in a salad? It's not only tasty, but it can be exciting when used with authentic Italian generosity in mind. The idea of this recipe is to inspire you to get creative with different ingredients. Try smoked ham, blue cheese, and thinly sliced Tuscan kale. This salad goes well with the Wise Guy Pizza (page 158).

1. Place the onion in a small bowl of ice water and let sit while you prepare the rest of the ingredients.

2. Remove and discard the outer leaves of the iceberg lettuce. Cut the lettuce in half through the core, then cut out and discard the core. Separate the lettuce leaves. Stack 2 or 3 leaves and cut them lengthwise into strips ¼ inch (5 mm) wide and then in half again. Place in a large salad bowl. Repeat with the remaining lettuce leaves. Thinly slice the radicchio the same way and add to the bowl. Cut the provolone and salami into strips ¼ inch (5 mm) wide and add to the bowl.

3. Drain the onion, pat dry with paper towels, and add to the salad. Add the cherry tomatoes, chickpeas, red peppers, parsley, and chili flakes. Season with salt and pepper and toss to combine well. Drizzle the House Vinaigrette over the salad, then sprinkle with the lemon juice; toss gently to coat the salad evenly.

4. Transfer the salad to a large platter or divide it among individual plates, piling it high. Sprinkle with the dried basil and serve.

½ small red onion, diced

1 large head iceberg lettuce

1 head radicchio

4 ounces (115 g) sliced provolone cheese

4 ounces (115 g) sliced salami

1 pint (500 mL) sweet cherry tomatoes, halved

1 can (14 ounces/398 g) chickpeas, drained and rinsed

3 sweet red peppers, roasted, peeled, and thinly sliced

2 tablespoons (30 mL) chopped fresh flat-leaf parsley

1½ teaspoons (7 mL) red chili flakes

Kosher salt and freshly ground pepper

6 tablespoons (90 mL) House Vinaigrette (page 244)

Juice of 1 lemon

1 tablespoon (15 mL) dried basil

KALE CAESAR SALAD

We started serving this salad with Tuscan black kale cut into thin strips, which made for a chewier salad that our customers had a love-hate relationship with. When we tried it with these baby greens, it was a hit, and so baby kale it is. White anchovies are lightly salted and packed in vinegar and have a fresh, tangy flavour we prefer in salads. Brown anchovies are packed in salt, which gives then a stronger flavour best used in cooked dishes. This salad goes well with the Umami Burger (page 112) or as an appetizer before our Pork Chops with Sage and Balsamic Vinegar (page 184).

½ loaf rustic white bread
½ cup (125 mL) olive oil
3 tablespoons (45 mL) fresh thyme, minced
6 cups (1.5 L) packed baby kale
⅓ cup (75 mL) Caesar Salad Dressing (page 245)
⅓ cup (75 mL) grated Parmesan cheese
Kosher salt and freshly ground pepper
8 thin slices bacon, chopped and cooked until crisp
Grated zest and juice of 1 lemon
6 white anchovies

1. Preheat the oven to 400°F (200°C). Line a baking sheet with parchment paper.

2. To make the croutons, cut the bread in half and pull the soft bread out of the centre of the loaf, leaving the crust behind. Tear the soft bread into bite-size pieces. You should have about 3 cups (750 mL). Spread the bread pieces on the prepared baking sheet, drizzle with olive oil, scatter over the thyme, and toss well. Spread in a single layer and bake for about 12 minutes, until golden and crisp. Let cool.

3. In a large salad bowl, combine the kale, half the croutons, half the Caesar Salad Dressing, and half the Parmesan; toss well. Taste and season with salt and pepper; toss with more dressing if needed. Add the remaining croutons, the bacon, and lemon juice; toss again. Sprinkle the remaining Parmesan and the lemon zest over the salad, garnish with the anchovies, and serve.

ROASTED ASPARAGUS WITH MANCHEGO CHEESE

SERVES 4 TO 6

We are frequently asked which is better—fat asparagus spears or the skinny ones. We like the fat ones. Fat asparagus is juicier and has a meaty texture, giving it the heft to stand up to grilling or roasting. Spanish Manchego is one of our favourite cheeses. It has a unique nutty flavour. Look for a Manchego that has the Protected Designation of Origin (PDO) label. This is an assurance that the cheese is very high quality and authentic. It is worth the cost. This dish makes a nice spring lunch paired with the Campfire-Style Rainbow Trout (page 196).

1. Remove the tough ends of the asparagus with a knife. In a medium bowl, toss the asparagus with the olive oil and a pinch or two of salt.

2. Heat a large skillet over medium-high heat. Working in batches, carefully add enough asparagus to the hot skillet to make one layer. Give them a shake to ensure each spear comes in contact with the pan—this will ensure that the asparagus gets some colour. After 3 minutes, roll them over and cook for an additional 5 minutes, rolling the asparagus a few times. You want them charred and slightly soft but not crunchy-raw.

3. Arrange the asparagus on a platter and sprinkle with the chives, parsley, and lemon zest. Season with salt and pepper. Scatter over the Manchego cheese shavings and serve.

3 pounds (1.35 kg) asparagus (about 3 big bundles)
2 tablespoons (30 mL) olive oil
Kosher salt and freshly ground pepper
1 tablespoon (15 mL) chopped fresh chives
1 tablespoon (15 mL) chopped fresh flat-leaf parsley
1 tablespoon (15 mL) grated lemon zest
5 ounces (140 g) Spanish Manchego cheese, shaved with a vegetable peeler

QUINOA, CHICKPEA, AND BLACK BEAN SALAD

SERVES 4 TO 6

This is our most popular salad and a permanent offering on the menu. This salad is as healthy as it gets. Beans, grains, and legumes, packed full of protein, fibre, and flavour. The jalapeño pesto is a bolt of heat that can be adjusted to your taste. Our cooks can be heavy handed with it, but our customers love it! This salad goes well with the Corn and Poblano Soup (page 30).

---

1. In a large bowl, combine the quinoa, arugula, black beans, chickpeas, green onions, lime zest, and Jalapeño Pesto. Drizzle the House Vinaigrette over the salad; toss gently to coat the salad evenly. Season with salt and pepper.

2. Transfer the salad to a large platter or divide it among individual plates, piling it high. Sprinkle with the feta and Crispy Quinoa.

3½ cups (875 mL) cooked white quinoa
2 cups (500 mL) packed baby arugula
½ cup (125 mL) canned black beans, rinsed
½ cup (125 mL) canned chickpeas, rinsed
¼ cup (60 mL) chopped green onions
2 tablespoons (30 mL) grated lime zest
1 tablespoon (15 mL) Jalapeño Pesto
   (page 258)
⅓ cup (75 mL) House Vinaigrette
   (page 244)
Kosher salt and freshly ground pepper
4 ounces (115 g) feta cheese, crumbled
¼ cup (60 mL) Crispy Quinoa (page 252)

PEACH AND MOZZARELLA SALAD

Summer is the time to enjoy peaches. We love peaches, and when they are perfectly ripe, we love to simply eat them over the kitchen sink. Unfortunately, that sweet moment is elusive, so this recipe is designed to make the almost ripe, not-quite-there-yet peach taste spectacular. This salad would also look good draped with some thin slices of prosciutto. We serve this with our Buttermilk Fried Chicken (page 171).

6 peaches, each sliced into 6 wedges

¼ cup (60 mL) sugar

½ teaspoon (2 mL) kosher salt

2 tablespoons (30 mL) extra-virgin olive oil

¼ cup (60 mL) almonds, toasted and coarsely chopped

1 teaspoon (5 mL) cumin seeds, toasted

5 fresh mint leaves, torn

5 fresh basil leaves, torn

Kosher salt and freshly ground pepper

6 ounces (170 g) fresh mozzarella cheese, torn into bite-size pieces

1. In a medium bowl, toss the peach wedges with the sugar and salt. Let sit for at least 15 minutes, though 1 hour is better. This will create a bit of peachy nectar that acts like a dressing for the salad.

2. Add the olive oil, almonds, cumin seeds, mint, and basil. Season with salt and pepper and toss gently to coat.

3. Transfer to a platter and evenly distribute the cheese in and around the peaches.

SPICY LENTIL, WILD RICE, AND ORZO SALAD

SERVES 6

This is a variation of a family favourite. We tend to change it up each time we make it, based on what is available at the market. For example, in summer we add sweet cherry tomatoes or steamed corn, while in winter, we add roasted squash. The aroma of wild rice as it cooks is amazing—kind of like fresh hay on a hot summer day. This salad goes well with the Tomato Soup with Fried Chickpeas (page 39) or as a first course before Apple Bacon Pizza (page 143).

1. In a medium pot, bring the rice and 4 cups (1 L) water to a boil; reduce the heat, cover, and simmer until most of the rice is split and tender, about 45 minutes. Remove from the heat and let stand, covered, for 10 minutes. Drain if necessary, then set aside.

2. In the same pot (or at the same time in another pot), bring 6 cups (1.5 L) lightly salted water to a boil. Add the orzo and stir. Boil the orzo for about 10 minutes, or until it has a firm, chewy texture. Drain and rinse under cold water, then set aside.

3. In a small pot, bring 1½ cups (375 mL) lightly salted water to a boil. Add the green lentils and stir. Boil the lentils for about 20 minutes, or until tender. Drain and rinse under cold water, then set aside.

4. In a large bowl, stir together the House Vinaigrette, cayenne, coriander, cumin, turmeric, and cinnamon. Stir in the rice, orzo, lentils, and cilantro. Season with salt and pepper.

5. Tip out onto a platter and evenly distribute the cashews in and around the salad. Drizzle the lemon juice over the top and serve.

1 cup (250 mL) wild rice, rinsed
1 cup (250 mL) orzo
½ cup (125 mL) green lentils, rinsed
¼ cup (60 mL) House Vinaigrette (page 244)
1 teaspoon (5 mL) cayenne pepper
1 teaspoon (5 mL) ground coriander
1 teaspoon (5 mL) ground cumin
½ teaspoon (2 mL) turmeric
¼ teaspoon (1 mL) cinnamon
½ cup (125 mL) chopped fresh cilantro
Kosher salt and freshly ground pepper
½ cup (125 mL) chopped unsalted cashews, for garnish
Juice of 1 lemon, for garnish

COLESLAW

SERVES 8 • REQUIRES TIME FOR PREP

Coleslaw does not get the respect it deserves. Can you imagine summer without this versatile salad? A perfect combination of creamy, tart, and crunchy. We often serve it alongside our Buttermilk Fried Chicken (page 171), and it also goes well with our Porchetta Sandwich (page 119).

8 cups (2 L) thinly sliced green cabbage

2 cups (500 mL) thinly sliced red cabbage

1 red onion, thinly sliced

1 tablespoon (15 mL) kosher salt

⅓ cup (75 mL) Basic Mayonnaise (page 246) or store-bought

⅓ cup (75 mL) plain full-fat yogurt

3 tablespoons (45 mL) unseasoned rice vinegar

1 tablespoon (15 mL) sugar

12 fresh mint leaves, finely chopped

1 teaspoon (5 mL) minced fresh thyme

1 teaspoon (5 mL) minced fresh flat-leaf parsley

Grated zest and juice of 1 lemon

Kosher salt and freshly ground pepper

1. In a large bowl, toss together the green and red cabbages, onion, and salt. Let stand for 1 hour.

2. In a colander, drain the cabbage mixture. Squeeze out excess moisture with your hands and return the cabbage mixture to the bowl.

3. In a medium bowl, whisk together the Basic Mayonnaise, yogurt, rice vinegar, sugar, mint, thyme, parsley, lemon zest and juice, and salt and pepper to taste. Add the mayonnaise mixture to the cabbage mixture and toss to mix well. Cover and refrigerate for 1 hour.

4. Serve chilled on the same day.

FRENCH CARROT SALAD

SERVES 4 TO 6 • REQUIRES TIME FOR PREP

The curry-like Vadouvan Spice Blend (page 266) is the magic ingredient. This salad is wonderful as part of a buffet alongside Roasted Eggplant with Miso and Green Peppers (page 65) and the Heirloom Tomato Salad (page 58).

6 large carrots, peeled

Leaves from ½ bunch fresh flat-leaf parsley, chopped

3 tablespoons (45 mL) Vadouvan Spice Blend (page 266) or store-bought

⅓ cup (75 mL) House Vinaigrette (page 244)

Kosher salt and freshly ground pepper

¼ cup (60 mL) plain full-fat yogurt, for garnish

1. Grate the carrots in fine shreds using a box grater, and place in a medium salad bowl. Add the parsley, Vadouvan Spice Blend, and House Vinaigrette and toss well to combine. Season to taste with salt and pepper. Chill the salad for 1 hour for the flavours to mellow.

2. Serve cold, topped with yogurt.

ROASTED EGGPLANT WITH MISO AND GREEN PEPPERS

SERVES 4 TO 6

We are always dreaming up things to do with all the different types of eggplant that are so plentiful in summer. When we grow tired of Italian or French flavours at Bread Bar, we set our sights on Japan. Miso paste has an addictive mellowness and depth of fermented flavour: loads of umami, salty-sweet. These eggplant wedges don't fully keep their shape once they're roasted, so don't worry if the result looks a little mushy. You can replace the miso paste with 2 tablespoons (30 mL) Za'atar Spice Blend (page 265) or 1 tablespoon (15 mL) Vadouvan Spice Blend (page 244).

1. Preheat the oven to 400°F (200°C).

2. Cut the eggplants in half lengthwise. Score the flesh of each half with deep diagonal crisscross cuts, making sure not to pierce the skin.

3. Heat the canola oil in a medium ovenproof skillet over medium heat. Add the eggplant halves cut side down and fry until the cut side is crispy and golden, about 5 minutes. Remove from the heat.

4. In a small bowl, stir together the miso, sugar, and water to make a loose paste. Turn the eggplants over and smear the miso paste over the cut sides. Nestle the green peppers between and around the eggplants. Roast for 30 minutes, or until the eggplants and green peppers are soft.

5. Arrange the eggplants and green peppers on a platter and season with salt and pepper. Scatter the cilantro over top and sprinkle with a generous squeeze of lime. Serve immediately.

2 medium Italian eggplants
3 tablespoons (45 mL) canola oil
⅓ cup (75 mL) white miso paste
1 tablespoon (15 mL) sugar
2 tablespoons (30 mL) water
1 medium green bell pepper, seeded and cut into 10 lengthwise slices
Kosher salt and freshly ground pepper
3 tablespoons (45 mL) chopped fresh cilantro, for garnish
1 or 2 limes, halved, for garnish

GREEN BEANS WITH MISO DRESSING

SERVES 4

Variations of classic dishes are not about changing things up entirely. It's more about respecting the original idea of a dish while kicking up the flavours where we can. Here, French green bean salad meets Japan. This dish goes well with Pork Chops with Sage and Balsamic Vinegar (page 184) and the Roasted Swordfish with Umami Sauce (page 203).

---

1. Steam the green beans for 3 minutes, or until bright green and slightly crisp.

2. Heat the olive oil in a medium skillet over medium-high heat. Add the beans, garlic, and cherry tomatoes. Sauté, stirring frequently, for 2 minutes. Remove from the heat.

3. Add the lemon zest, sesame seeds, and Miso Dressing; toss well. Season with salt and pepper if needed. Serve warm.

1 pound (450 g) green beans, trimmed

2 tablespoons (30 mL) extra-virgin olive oil

1 clove garlic, chopped

1 pint (500 mL) cherry tomatoes, halved

2 teaspoons (10 mL) grated lemon zest

2 teaspoons (10 mL) black or white sesame seeds

2 tablespoons (30 mL) Miso Dressing (page 245)

Kosher salt and freshly ground pepper

ASPARAGUS WITH GREEN GODDESS DRESSING

SERVES 4

We love dishes with catchy names. Green goddess dressing is a California classic from the 1920s. Its herbaceous flavour is a perfect match for asparagus. Once this dressing is in your repertoire, you'll find yourself using it for all sorts of things, like we do. Try serving it with the Campfire-Style Rainbow Trout (page 196) or the Quinoa Super-Star Veggie Burger (page 115).

---

1 bunch asparagus, trimmed and cut into 1½-inch (4 cm) pieces

1 cup (250 mL) fresh or thawed frozen green peas

2 heads Bibb lettuce, leaves separated

1 tablespoon (15 mL) Quick Pickled Shallots (page 254)

6 fresh chives, cut into 1-inch (2.5 cm) lengths

5 fresh mint leaves, chopped

1 tablespoon (15 mL) chopped fresh dill

3 tablespoons (45 mL) House Vinaigrette (page 244)

Kosher salt and freshly ground pepper

3 tablespoons (45 mL) Green Goddess Dressing (page 244)

1. Bring a medium saucepan of water to a boil. Carefully drop in the asparagus and cook for 4 minutes. Remove the asparagus and plunge it into an ice water bath to stop the cooking. Drain and set aside. If you are using fresh peas, repeat, cooking them for only 2 minutes. Pat dry the asparagus and peas. (If using frozen peas, only defrost them.)

2. In a medium salad bowl, combine the asparagus, peas, lettuce, Quick Pickled Shallots, chives, mint, dill, and House Vinaigrette. Season with salt and pepper and gently toss. Drizzle with the Green Goddess Dressing and serve.

TACO SALAD

SERVES 4 TO 6

We have fond memories of taco night as kids. Nothing fancy, just the hard store-bought shells stuffed with ground beef, spiced using the package that came with the taco kit. As adults, what really sparks the memory is what remains on the plate after you've eaten a few tacos—a mess of crispy shell bits, cheese, beans, and lettuce. This is the inspiration for our Taco Salad. Try this with the Fried Chicken Sandwich (page 128).

1. Place the onion in a small bowl of ice water and let sit while you prepare the rest of the ingredients.

2. Remove and discard the outer leaves of the iceberg lettuce. Cut the lettuce in half through the core, then cut out and discard the core. Separate the lettuce leaves. Stack 2 or 3 leaves and cut them lengthwise into strips ¼ inch (5 mm) wide. Place in a large salad bowl. Repeat with the remaining lettuce leaves.

3. Drain the onion, pat dry with paper towels, and add to the lettuce. Add the cheese, Chipotle Black Beans, Salsa Rosa, pumpkin seeds, cilantro, lime juice, and chili flakes. Toss well, and season with salt and pepper if needed. Drizzle the House Vinaigrette over the salad, top with the Guacamole and crushed tortilla chips, and serve.

½ red onion, finely diced
1 large head iceberg lettuce
2 cups (500 mL) crumbled queso fresco cheese
1½ cups (375 mL) Chipotle Black Beans (page 251)
1 cup (250 mL) Salsa Rosa (page 257)
½ cup (125 mL) raw pumpkin seeds
2 tablespoons (30 mL) chopped fresh cilantro
2 tablespoons (30 mL) freshly squeezed lime juice
1½ teaspoons (7 mL) red chili flakes
Kosher salt and freshly ground pepper
6 tablespoons (90 mL) House Vinaigrette (page 244)

Toppings
1 cup (250 mL) Guacamole (page 256)
1 cup (250 mL) crushed crispy tortilla chips

SHARED APPETIZERS

PASS THE BREAD, PLEASE

Bettina's dogs are always happy to devour the dog food put in front of them. As she watches them happily eat the same meal day after day, she finds herself a bit reflective. For the average human, daily meals are not so simple. People have likes and dislikes, food allergies and intolerances, ethics and politics and religion. As well, we must navigate a swirl of competing scientific and anecdotal opinion that surrounds some modern food concerns. What should we eat versus what we want to eat versus what is available to us.

Food choices can be even more unnerving in a restaurant setting. Some of us are dedicated vegans or casual vegetarians; others are lactose-intolerant or following a gluten-free diet. The act of eating has become overly complicated, and at Bread Bar we knew we wanted to simplify it and make the experience an engaging one for all our customers. We want Bread Bar to be a fun place,

encouraging our customers to enjoy themselves and shed any food choice anxiety. That's why we spend our time focusing our efforts on coaxing the flavour out of the best ingredients we can find, while using traditional flavour pairings with contemporary accompaniments. Fun is the name of the game here, and one thing we've noticed is that our customers tend to enjoy their food more when it is passed around the table and shared. Perhaps that's why family-style meals are so popular in restaurants. There is even science to back this up.

A few years ago Bettina attended a talk given by Hervé This, the father of molecular gastronomy. His talk gave Bettina a great deal to think about, but the biggest takeaway was This's discussion of how eating together affects how we enjoy our food. In an experiment he devised to explore this idea, This brought four people together for dinner. In the first part of the experiment, each person ordered a different dish; afterwards, they described the meal as enjoyable. In the second part of the experiment, two of the four people shared the same dishes family-style and the other two ordered different dishes; this time the individuals rated the meal even more enjoyable than the first. In the third part, all four people shared the same dishes; this was the meal all four said they most enjoyed.

This is the kind of meal we try to create at Bread Bar. A large pizza shared between four inspires conversation and connection. And it's not uncommon for tables of two or four or six to order dishes to share. That includes pizzas and salads, and whole roasted lamb shoulders. We do offer shared plates on the menu, such as calamari, hummus, and a charcuterie board, but our customers seem to know intrinsically that sharing any dish is the most enjoyable way to have a meal.

Once the food arrives, a comfortable quiet can settle over the table. Some customers linger over their meal; others don't chat until every morsel is gone from the plate. It's not an awkward atmosphere but a pleasant one, one that indicates enjoyment. Service staff have noted how tough it can be to interrupt a table once the food arrives. Customers just want to enjoy the food and connect with the people with whom they are eating. A shared meal is the best meal, and it's that feeling of connection that draws you back.

BLISTERED PADRÓN PEPPERS
WITH BASIL AND PINE NUT MAYONNAISE

Eating Padrón, or shishito, peppers is also know as Spanish roulette, since about one in ten is very hot! The exciting part is that it's pretty much impossible to tell which one until you put it in your mouth. The best way to prepare these chilies is to give them searing heat on a grill or hot cast-iron pan. We prefer the subtle smoke of a grill for this dish. The mayonnaise adds a cooling richness to these chilies. The dish goes well with the Green Goddess Pizza (page 244) or as an appetizer before Piri Piri Baby Back Ribs (page 176).

1. Preheat a grill pan or outdoor grill to medium-high. Meanwhile, place the peppers in a medium bowl, add the olive oil, and toss to coat.

2. Place the peppers on the hot grill in a single layer, making sure they aren't touching. Reserve the bowl. Grill the peppers, uncovered and turning them occasionally, until they start to char and blister, about 6 minutes.

3. Return the peppers to the bowl, immediately add salt to taste, and toss. Serve hot with Garlic Confit and Basil and Pine Nut Mayonnaise in bowls on the side.

½ pound (225 g) Padrón peppers
1 tablespoon (15 mL) olive oil
Coarse sea salt, such as Maldon
10 cloves Garlic Confit (page 253)
½ cup (125 mL) Basil and Pine Nut Mayonnaise (page 249)

GRILLED OCTOPUS WITH POTATOES AND MINT

SERVES 4 TO 6 · REQUIRES TIME FOR PREP

Octopus can be tricky to cook—if you let it boil, it will toughen. Simmering it gently, in an aromatic broth, helps it to become tender. Potatoes are a traditional Spanish accompaniment to octopus, and we find they add an earthy balance to this dish. Share this as an appetizer before our Roasted Swordfish with Umami Sauce (page 203).

1 thawed frozen octopus (2½ pounds/
    1.125 kg)—freezing tenderizes the octopus
1 fennel bulb, chopped
1 white onion, chopped
2 celery stalks, chopped
3 cloves garlic, chopped
1 tablespoon (15 mL) coriander seeds
1 tablespoon (15 mL) red chili flakes
2 cups (500 mL) dry white wine or water
Kosher salt and freshly ground pepper
12 mini potatoes
3 tablespoons (45 mL) olive oil
1 cup (250 mL) plain full-fat yogurt
2 tablespoons (30 mL) chopped fresh mint
1 long red chili, seeded and chopped
Grated zest and juice of 1 lemon

1. Preheat the oven to 300°F (150°C).

2. In a large Dutch oven, combine the octopus, fennel, onion, celery, garlic, coriander seeds, chili flakes, white wine, and salt to taste. Cover and slowly bring to a simmer over medium-low heat. Place in the oven and cook until the octopus is easily pierced with a knife, about 1½ hours. Remove from the oven and let the octopus cool in the liquid.

3. Remove the octopus, discarding the cooking liquid and vegetables. Using scissors, separate the tentacles from the body. Cut the head above the eyes and beak, discard the eyes and beak. Cut the remaining head portion into 1-inch (2.5 cm) squares. Combine the tentacles and the head in a bowl. Set aside.

4. In a large pot of salted water, bring the potatoes to a boil over high heat and cook until easily pierced with a knife, about 15 minutes. Drain the potatoes. Slightly flatten each potato under your thumb, keeping them mostly intact. Season with salt and pepper.

5. To finish the dish, heat the olive oil in a large skillet over high heat. Add the octopus and potatoes, working in batches if they don't all fit. Sear the octopus and potatoes for 2 minutes on each side to get a good crust.

6. Drizzle the yogurt onto a platter, then evenly distribute the octopus and potatoes on the platter. Sprinkle with the mint, chili, and lemon zest. Season with salt and pepper. Drizzle with a splash of olive oil and lemon juice. Serve immediately.

TOAST FOUR WAYS

We prefer to toast only one side of our bread, which gives it a complex bite, one side crispy while the other is soft. These recipes will be a great addition to your cooking repertoire. Each topping would also be delicious on pastas or backyard burgers or as a filling for lunch sandwiches. Try the Roasted Corn Salsa on our Margherita Pizza (page 140).

1. Heat a medium skillet over medium heat. Brush the olive oil over one side of each bread slice and place the slices, oiled side down, in a single layer in the skillet. Fry for 2 minutes, or until the bottom is crispy and toasty brown. Season the crispy side with salt and pepper and pile on the topping of your choice.

2 tablespoons (30 mL) olive oil

8 slices baguette or Steeltown Crusty Bread (page 15), each ¾ inch (2 cm) thick

Kosher salt and freshly ground pepper

ROASTED CORN SALSA

1. Clean the corn of its husk and silk. Using a sharp knife, cut the kernels from the cob.

2. Heat the olive oil in a medium skillet over medium-high heat. Add the corn kernels and sauté until the corn is slightly charred, about 8 minutes. Remove from the heat and let cool.

3. In a medium bowl, combine the corn, onion, tomatoes, jalapeño peppers, cilantro, cheese, and lime juice; mix well. Season with salt and pepper.

4. Spread the mixture over each slice of fried bread and serve.

1 ear corn

1 tablespoon (15 mL) olive oil

½ small white onion, finely chopped

1 pound (450 g) ripe tomatoes, peeled, seeded, and finely chopped

2 small jalapeño peppers, seeded and minced

½ cup (125 mL) chopped fresh cilantro

½ cup (125 mL) crumbled queso fresco or feta cheese

2 tablespoons (30 mL) freshly squeezed lime juice

Kosher salt and freshly ground pepper

SPICY SHRIMP SALAD

REQUIRES TIME FOR PREP

⅔ cup (150 mL) Basic Mayonnaise
  (page 246) or store-bought
¼ cup (60 mL) plain full-fat yogurt
1 tablespoon (15 mL) finely chopped fresh
  tarragon
1½ teaspoons (7 mL) red wine vinegar
1 pound (450 g) cooked mini salad shrimp
½ cup (125 mL) finely chopped celery
¼ cup (60 mL) finely chopped white onion
1 tablespoon (15 mL) capers, minced
¼ teaspoon (1 mL) cayenne pepper
¼ teaspoon (1 mL) smoked paprika
Kosher salt and freshly ground pepper

1. In a medium bowl, stir together the Basic Mayonnaise, yogurt, tarragon, and red wine vinegar.

2. Add the shrimp, celery, onion, capers, cayenne, and paprika; mix well. Season with salt and pepper. Chill for at least 1 hour.

3. Spread the mixture over each slice of fried bread slice and serve.

MASHED PEAS WITH MINT AND PROSCIUTTO

1 cup (250 mL) water
1¼ teaspoons (6 mL) kosher salt, divided
1½ pounds (675 g) fresh or frozen green
  peas
3 tablespoons (45 mL) unsalted butter, cut
  into ½-inch (1 cm) cubes, softened
¼ cup (60 mL) minced fresh mint
1 tablespoon (15 mL) chopped fresh flat-
  leaf parsley
Juice of 1 lemon
4 thin slices high-quality prosciutto, cut
  into equal halves

1. Bring the water and ¼ teaspoon (1 mL) of the salt to a boil in a medium pot. Add the peas and cook, stirring occasionally, until heated through and tender, about 5 minutes.

2. While the peas cook, in a small bowl stir together the butter, mint, parsley, and the remaining 1 teaspoon (5 mL) salt until well combined.

3. Transfer the peas with their cooking water to a food processor and pulse until coarsely puréed. Transfer to a medium bowl. Add the herb butter and stir until well blended and smooth. Add the lemon juice. Taste and adjust seasoning with more salt or lemon juice.

4. Spread the mixture over each slice of fried bread, top with a slice of prosciutto, and serve.

PORCINI MUSHROOMS

REQUIRES TIME FOR PREP

1. Place the dried porcini mushrooms in a small bowl and cover with warm water. Let sit for 20 minutes, or until soft. Strain through a fine-mesh sieve, reserving the liquid. Chop the softened porcini mushrooms.

2. Heat the olive oil in a large skillet over high heat. Add the porcini mushrooms, button mushrooms, enoki mushrooms, onion, garlic, and water. Sauté until the mushrooms are dry and sizzling, about 15 minutes. Add the reserved porcini mushroom liquid and cook until the mushrooms are again dry. Stir in the cream, bring to a boil, then reduce the heat and simmer until the cream has thickened.

3. Remove from the heat and add 2 tablespoons (30 mL) of the Parmesan, the parsley, and salt and pepper to taste; stir well. Let cool.

4. Spread the mixture over each slice of fried bread. Garnish with the remaining 1 tablespoon (15 mL) Parmesan and serve.

1½ ounces (40 g) dried porcini mushrooms
1 tablespoon (15 mL) olive oil
1½ pounds (675 g) small button mushrooms, sliced
1 cup (250 mL) enoki mushrooms
1 small red onion, chopped
1 clove garlic, minced
2 tablespoons (30 mL) water
1 cup (250 mL) heavy (35%) cream
3 tablespoons (45 mL) grated Parmesan cheese, divided
2 tablespoons (30 mL) chopped fresh flat-leaf parsley
Salt and freshly ground pepper

DEVILS ON HORSEBACK

MAKES 15 PIECES • REQUIRES TIME FOR PREP

We serve these bacon-wrapped prunes at Bread Bar in the fall and winter as a shared appetizer. Customers love this salty, sweet, and smoky snack paired with seasonal cocktails or wine. If you have any leftover glaze, try it drizzled over our Coconut Cranberry Granola (page 207) for breakfast.

1 cup (250 mL) water
1 cup (250 mL) dry red wine (or port, but omit the sugar)
1 tablespoon (15 mL) sugar
15 large prunes, pitted
4 ounces (115 g) blue cheese
15 thin slices bacon, each 4 inches (10 cm) long

1. In a small saucepan, combine the water, red wine, sugar and prunes. The prunes should be completely submerged; if they are not, add more red wine. Bring to a boil, then reduce the heat and simmer for 15 minutes. Remove from the heat and let the prunes sit in the liquid for at least 2 hours and preferably overnight. Remove the prunes, reserving the liquid.

2. Using your fingers, break off some blue cheese and carefully stuff the prunes. This is not an exact science, so do your best. The prunes should be full, but not messy with cheese, as the cheese could burn during the cooking.

3. Put a prune at one end of a slice of bacon and roll up so the prune is wrapped in the bacon. Skewer the prune with a toothpick through the end of the bacon to keep the bacon tight. Repeat with all the prunes.

4. Heat a medium skillet over medium heat until hot. Add the bacon-wrapped prunes, and cook, carefully turning occasionally, until the bacon is crisp and the prunes are hot, about 8 minutes. Transfer to a serving plate.

5. Add ¼ cup (60 mL) of the reserved red wine mixture to the hot pan, swirling the pan until the liquid is reduced to a syrupy glaze. Pour over the bacon-wrapped prunes and serve immediately.

GENERAL TSO'S FRIED CAULIFLOWER

SERVES 4 TO 6

When we first envisioned Bread Bar, we knew that our community was going to help write the menu. Sure enough, our customers often requested modern vegetarian dishes. We developed this dish to appeal to the meat eater as well. It has the same sweet and tangy quality as the classic chicken dish, but vegetarian. When buying cauliflower, look for compact, dense heads, preferably with fresh-looking, unwilted leaves. This dish goes well with Roasted Salmon and Seaweed Rice Bowls (page 200).

1. To make the sauce, in a small bowl stir together the water and cornstarch to make a smooth slurry. Add the chicken stock, tomato paste, rice vinegar, and soy sauce; stir until smooth. Set aside.

2. Bring a large pot of water to a boil. Add the salt, then carefully add the cauliflower. Boil until the cauliflower is fork-tender, about 8 minutes. Drain well and let cool completely.

3. Pour 3½ cups (875 mL) canola oil into a large wok, or enough oil to rise 1½ inches (4 cm) from the bottom. Set over high heat until the oil reaches 350°F (180°C).

4. In a large bowl, toss the cauliflower in the flour, shaking off excess. Carefully add half the cauliflower to the wok and fry until crisp and deep gold in colour, about 3 minutes. Using a slotted spoon, transfer the cauliflower to a plate lined with paper towel. Repeat with the second batch. Pour the canola oil into a heatproof container and wipe out the wok.

5. Return the wok to high heat. Add the remaining 3 tablespoons (45 mL) canola oil. When hot, add the chilies and stir-fry for a few seconds, until they just start to change colour. Add the garlic and ginger and stir-fry for a few seconds longer, until fragrant. Add the sauce, stirring as it thickens. Return the cauliflower to the wok and stir vigorously to coat. Remove from the heat, stir in the sesame oil and garnish with green onions and chopped peanuts. Serve with steamed rice.

Sauce
1 tablespoon (15 mL) water
½ teaspoon (2 mL) cornstarch
3 tablespoons (45 mL) chicken stock or water
1 tablespoon (15 mL) tomato paste
1 tablespoon (15 mL) unseasoned rice vinegar
2 teaspoons (10 mL) soy sauce

Fried Cauliflower
1 tablespoon (15 mL) kosher salt
2 medium heads cauliflower, cut into large florets
3½ cups (875 mL) + 3 tablespoons (45 mL) canola oil, divided
2 tablespoons (30 mL) all-purpose flour
2 whole Thai chilies
2 cloves garlic, minced
2 teaspoons (10 mL) minced fresh ginger
1 teaspoon (5 mL) sesame oil

Garnishes
2 green onions, thinly sliced
¼ cup (60 mL) chopped roasted peanuts

CRISPY BRUSSELS SPROUTS WITH UMAMI SAUCE

SERVES 4

We all have New York chef David Chang of Momofuku to thank for making Brussels sprouts hot sellers.
If not for him, we would have never fried a handful one night and had our minds blown.
These go well with the Roasted Mushroom Pizza (page 150).

1 pound (450 g) Brussels sprouts, trimmed

1 cup (250 mL) chopped bacon

1 cup (250 mL) canola oil

1 apple, cored and thinly sliced (we use Cortland)

1 tablespoon (15 mL) sesame seeds

2 teaspoons (10 mL) red chili flakes

2 teaspoons (10 mL) kosher salt

2 tablespoons (30 mL) Umami Sauce (page 264)

1. Cut the Brussels sprouts in half lengthwise. Set aside.

2. Heat a large, heavy skillet over high heat. Add the bacon and cook until crispy, stirring frequently, about 10 minutes. Using a slotted spoon, remove the bacon and set aside. Drain off the bacon fat and wipe out the skillet.

3. Heat the canola oil in the skillet over medium-high heat. When the oil is just short of smoking, carefully place the Brussels sprouts cut side down in the oil. Reduce the heat to medium and sear on one side until nicely browned, about 3 minutes. Turn the sprouts over and cook on the other side until nicely browned and tender, 3 to 5 minutes. Some of the leaves will be charred dark brown or black, which is fine. Drain the Brussels sprouts on paper towels. Transfer to a medium serving bowl.

4. Add the bacon, apple, sesame seeds, chili flakes, and salt; toss gently to mix. Serve drizzled with Umami Sauce.

FRIED CALAMARI

SERVES 4 TO 6

For as long as we can remember, fried calamari has been a staple of every bar and restaurant, whether Italian themed or not. It is a great snack or light dinner when you make it at home yourself. For best results, especially for that delectable crispy coating, eat these as soon as they're made. We serve our calamari with Chili Confit (page 253) and Thai Chili Mayonnaise (page 248) as garnishes.

1. Cut the tentacles from the squid, leaving them whole, and cut the bodies crosswise into ½-inch (1 cm) rings. Place the rings and tentacles in a medium bowl and cover with the buttermilk; allow to soak for about 10 minutes.

2. In a separate medium bowl, combine the flour and panko crumbs.

3. Drain the squid in a colander and shake gently to remove excess liquid. Gently dip the squid pieces into the flour mixture, pressing down with your hands and coating evenly. Remove them to a plate.

4. Heat the canola oil in a medium skillet over high heat. Working in batches so you don't crowd the pan, carefully add the squid rings and tentacles to the oil—they will spit and spatter. The calamari should be in one layer so each piece is in contact with the oil. Fry for 2 minutes, turning occasionally. Add some of the chorizo and fry for another 1 minute. Using a slotted spoon, transfer the calamari and chorizo to a medium bowl lined with a paper towel. Repeat with the remaining calamari and chorizo.

5. Remove the paper towel, add the parsley, lemon juice, and salt and pepper to taste and toss well. Serve immediately.

8 fresh squid, cleaned
2 cups (500 mL) buttermilk
1 cup (250 mL) all-purpose flour
1 cup (250 mL) panko crumbs
3 cups (750 mL) canola oil
1 cured chorizo sausage (3 ounces/85 g), cut into 8 pieces
1 tablespoon (15 mL) fresh flat-leaf parsley
1 tablespoon (15 mL) freshly squeezed lemon juice
Kosher salt and freshly ground pepper

MUSHROOM TARTS WITH TALEGGIO CHEESE

MAKES FOUR 5-INCH (12 CM) TARTS •
REQUIRES TIME FOR PREP

We both have a fondness for savoury baked dishes. Free-form tarts like these ones are quite easy to make, come together in no time, and never fail to impress. It is important that the mushrooms cook until dry in the skillet, to keep the pastry from getting soggy. We like to serve these tarts at brunch, but they also make for a satisfying lunch paired with our Butternut Squash Soup (page 29).

---

1 batch Basic Pie Dough, made with
   1 teaspoon (5 mL) pepper added to the
   dry ingredients (page 231)
¼ cup (60 mL) olive oil
1 white onion, diced
1 pound (450 g) assorted mushrooms,
   coarsely chopped
2 cloves garlic, minced
3 fresh sage leaves
Kosher salt
3 ounces (85 g) thinly sliced Taleggio
   cheese
1 egg, beaten

1. Divide the dough into 4 equal portions. On a lightly floured work surface, roll out one portion of the dough to ¼-inch (5 mm) thickness and trim it into a 6-inch (15 cm) square. Repeat with the remaining portions of dough, stacking the squares separated by parchment paper on a plate. Wrap the pastry in plastic and put back in the refrigerator to chill for at least 30 minutes or up to 3 days. (The pastry can also be frozen for up to 1 month.)

2. Preheat the oven to 400°F (200°C). Line a baking sheet with parchment paper.

3. Heat the olive oil in a medium skillet over high heat. Reduce the heat to medium, add the onion, and cook, stirring occasionally, until the onions are translucent and tender, about 10 minutes. Add the mushrooms, garlic, sage leaves, and a sprinkle of salt. Increase the heat to high and cook the mushrooms, stirring occasionally, for about 6 minutes, or until the mushrooms are dry and sizzling. Remove from the heat and let cool. Remove the sage leaves and discard.

4. Cut the Taleggio slices into 1-inch (2.5 cm) squares. Set aside.

5. Remove the dough from the refrigerator, arrange the squares on the prepared baking sheet, and allow to warm up just enough that the dough is pliable, about 10 minutes.

6. Spread the mushroom mixture evenly on the tarts, stopping about 1 inch (2.5 cm) from the edges. Top the mushrooms with the cheese squares. Brush the edges of the dough with the beaten egg, then fold the edges up around the mushrooms, leaving the centre open. Press the edges lightly to ensure they stay folded. Brush the outside of the dough with the remaining beaten egg. Bake until crust is golden brown, about 25 minutes. Serve immediately.

CREAMY HUMMUS WITH FRIED CHICKPEAS

SERVES 6 TO 8

In this age of convenience food, hummus is not typically made from scratch. But we still prefer to make our own. It takes minutes to throw together, especially if you use canned chickpeas, and homemade hummus tastes so much better than store-bought that you'll never go back to buying ready-made. We serve this creamy hummus on top of the Quinoa Super-Star Veggie Burger (page 115).

1. In a food processor, combine the chickpeas, tahini, olive oil, garlic, lemon juice, paprika, cumin, and salt and pepper to taste. Process until smooth. Add a little cold water if needed to produce a smooth purée. Taste and adjust seasoning, adding more salt, pepper, or lemon juice if needed. Transfer the hummus to a serving dish.

2. Drizzle with olive oil, sprinkle with paprika and lemon zest, and garnish with Fried Chickpeas and parsley.

3. Hummus will keep, covered in the refrigerator, for about 1 week.

1 can (19 ounces/540 mL) chickpeas, rinsed
¼ cup (60 mL) tahini
¼ cup (60 mL) extra-virgin olive oil, plus more for garnish
2 cloves garlic, minced
Grated zest and juice of 2 lemons
1 tablespoon (15 mL) smoked paprika, plus more for garnish
1 teaspoon (5 mL) ground cumin
Kosher salt and freshly ground pepper
½ cup (125 mL) Fried Chickpeas (page 39), for garnish
Chopped fresh flat-leaf parsley, for garnish

BURRATA AND BLISTERED CHERRY TOMATOES

SERVES 6

This must be the simplest dish we serve, and one of the most indulgent. To preserve the flavour and texture of handcrafted burrata, we order it twice a week so we can serve it as fresh as possible. The combination of the fresh, creamy cheese and ripe summer tomatoes is nothing short of perfection. When our farm is bursting with sun-drenched tomatoes, our customers can't get enough of this dish. It goes well with Spaghetti Arrabbiata (page 190).

6 slices fresh bread (we use our Rosemary Focaccia, page 22)

5 tablespoons (75 mL) extra-virgin olive oil, divided

24 ripe cherry tomatoes

Kosher salt and freshly ground pepper

1 ball fresh burrata cheese (about 8 ounces/225 g)

1 lemon

1. Set an oven rack at the highest level and preheat the broiler.

2. Brush one side of the bread slices generously with olive oil and arrange on one side of a baking sheet.

3. In a medium bowl, toss the cherry tomatoes with 3 tablespoons (45 mL) of the olive oil and season with salt. Place the tomatoes on the baking sheet next to the bread.

4. Place the baking sheet under the broiler and broil until the bread is toasted and the tomatoes are blistered. Watch carefully, as they may be done at different times.

5. Cut the burrata into quarters, pull it into chunks with your fingers, and arrange on a serving platter. Divide the toast and the tomatoes among the cheese on the platter. Drizzle everything with more olive oil and a squeeze of fresh lemon juice. Serve immediately.

BURGERS AND SANDWICHES

FUN IN THE KITCHEN

Grocery day is Bettina's favourite day of the week, whether it's at a local farmers' market or a trusted grocery store. Taking her inspiration from the covers of food magazines, as well as snooping in other people's carts, this is when she gets to stroll through the aisles or market stands and think up ideas for lunches and dinners. However, she knows her enthusiasm isn't shared by everyone. A regular customer once confessed how stressful grocery shopping was for her. It turned out she didn't enjoy cooking, so trips to the grocery store were intimidating and overwhelming. Though we both understand how this kind of food frustration can bubble up—busy lives often leave little time for meal prep. Early on we decided to make sure we enjoyed every moment in the kitchen with our families.

The hospitality industry can be unforgiving, and restaurant work is hard: the hours are long, the work is physically demanding. In our own way, we take food very seriously at Bread Bar, but we don't take ourselves very seriously. We laugh and joke (all right, sometimes inappropriately) in a way that keeps everyone in good spirits. Numerous pranks have been committed in our Bread Bar kitchens—a wet chef jacket left to freeze stiff in the walk-in freezer (sorry, Bryan!), or favourite sneakers baked into loaves of bread (sorry, Manny!). Jeff once rubbed a hot chili pepper on the rim of Bettina's water glass. After a long dinner service, she reached for her cold glass of water. Bettina swears her lips are still buzzing! These are among the many harmless and probably juvenile moments we've enjoyed. The question is, how do you have this kind of fun at home, since others in your family may not appreciate frozen clothing or buzzing lips?

Bettina's advice to that anxious grocery-shopping customer was to first learn to cook two or three easy recipes to perfection. A simple chicken noodle soup or chili made from scratch can be extremely gratifying. If you have a handful of no-fail recipes that you know taste good, the whole experience will be less stressful and the entire cooking experience more enjoyable. You will know what ingredients you need to buy and the time it will take to prepare the recipe, and you won't be worrying whether it will end up as leftovers.

Once you find you can cook a few dishes with ease, the next step is to make some changes to these tried and true recipes. Challenge yourself. You may be pleasantly surprised. You can easily increase flavour to make the everyday a little bit more special. Add ground coffee beans to your favourite barbecue sauce, chop a tart apple into your mac and cheese, or make a curry ketchup for your backyard burger. We are always exploring how we can make things easier *and* more delicious, but the trick is to start with a foundation recipe. At Bread Bar we are always fooling around with grilled cheese, a menu staple. We swap out the cheddar for Brie, add sliced apple or pear, and obviously bacon makes everything taste better.

Finally, making your time in the kitchen enjoyable includes creating an environment you want to be in. That can include simple things such as the music you play while chopping the vegetables to inviting people over to share in the cooking experience. The Bread Bar kitchens always have music playing—most often too loud—but the tunes keep everyone motivated. When good music is playing, the job feels less like work and more like a party. We have learned that if the staff are having fun in our kitchens, they're going to work harder, stay longer, and maintain their composure in a crisis, such as when a take-out order gets misplaced and isn't ready when the customer arrives. They will enjoy coming in to work and they will carry that fun out the door with them after the job is done. For the home cook, bringing some levity and relaxation into the cooking of the family dinner spills over into conversation and connectivity, the very reasons we come together around the dinner table.

Even the practised home cook who enjoys cooking likes a break from the stove, so splurge on yourself occasionally and eat out at your favourite neighbourhood restaurant or an expensive one you've been wanting to visit. Order a bottle of wine or a dish you've never tasted before. Ask questions about unfamiliar ingredients, and take your time to savour the meal. You'll find yourself inspired by the creativity of the chefs, and you may even discover a new take on one of your favourite recipes at home. What's important is to find the joy in every delicious moment.

CHEESE BURGER

MAKES 8 BURGERS • REQUIRES TIME FOR PREP

Competition for the best burger these days has gone mad. Patties are stuffed with five kinds of cheese, piled high will shocking ingredients, slathered in exotic sauces. Except for our amazing Umami Burger (page 112), we believe less is more and that using top-quality ingredients lets the flavours speak for themselves. We add ground pork to our burger for fat and flavour. This burger goes well with our Tomato Soup with Fried Chickpeas (page 39) or the Taco Salad (page 79) on the side.

1. In a medium bowl, combine the beef, pork, onion purée, horseradish, Worcestershire, salt, and pepper. Mix well but without overworking (this would make the burgers tough and dry). Divide the burger mix into 8 equal portions and shape into patties. To make sure they are solid but not overworked, slap the patties back and forth between your hands a couple of times. Place the burgers on a parchment-lined plate and refrigerate, covered, for 1 to 2 hours.

2. Preheat a grill to medium-high.

3. Grill the burgers, turning frequently, for about 8 minutes, for medium doneness. Do not press down on the burgers while they are cooking or you will squeeze out vital juices.

4. Toast the hamburger buns on the grill. Place each burger on the bottom half of a bun and garnish burgers with cheddar, iceberg lettuce, JC's Burger Sauce, and slices of red onion. Serve immediately.

2 pounds (900 g) ground beef chuck
1 pound (450 g) ground pork
¾ cup (175 mL) puréed white onion (about 1 medium onion)
1 teaspoon (5 mL) prepared horseradish
1 teaspoon (5 mL) Worcestershire sauce
1 tablespoon (15 mL) kosher salt
1 teaspoon (5 mL) freshly ground pepper
8 hamburger buns, buttered on each half

Garnishes
8 slices sharp white cheddar cheese
Iceberg lettuce
JC's Burger Sauce (page 264)
Sliced red onion

UMAMI BURGER

MAKES 4 BURGERS

Celebrity chefs and foodies love to throw around the word *umami*. It makes us sound worldly. But umami is a real thing. We like to describe it as meaty, savoury, salty, and sweet all at once. Umami flavour can be found in mushrooms, Parmesan, truffle, soy sauce, and tomatoes. We've pack it all into this burger recipe.

---

4 Cheese Burger patties (page 111)
4 hamburger buns, buttered on each half

Parmesan Crisps
1/4 cup (60 mL) grated Parmesan cheese

Umami Mushrooms
3 tablespoons (45 mL) olive oil
4 cups (1 L) mixed mushrooms (button, shiitake, cremini, oyster, chanterelle), chopped
2 tablespoons (30 mL) water
2 tablespoons (30 mL) Umami Sauce (page 264)
1 tablespoon (15 mL) minced fresh thyme
1 tablespoon (15 mL) minced fresh chives
1 clove garlic, minced
Kosher salt and freshly ground pepper

Garnishes
3 tablespoons (45 mL) Truffle Mayonnaise (page 249)
3 tablespoons (45 mL) Quick Pickled Shallots (page 254)

1. Preheat the oven to 375°F (190°C). Line a baking sheet with parchment paper.

2. To make the Parmesan Crisps, on the baking sheet, spoon level tablespoons (15 mL) of Parmesan in mounds 4 inches (10 cm) apart, making 4 cheese mounds. Flatten each mound slightly with your fingers to form a 4-inch (10 cm) round. The cheese should be in a very thin layer, with a few holes here and there.

3. Bake until golden and crisp, about 10 minutes. Let cool for 2 minutes on the baking sheet, then use a metal spatula to carefully transfer each crisp (they are very delicate) to a rack. Let cool completely.

4. To make the Umami Mushrooms, heat the olive oil in a medium skillet over high heat. Add the mushrooms and water and cook, without stirring, for 8 minutes. Stir, then continue to cook, stirring frequently, until the mushrooms are dry, about 4 minutes. Remove from the heat and stir in the Umami Sauce, thyme, chives, and garlic. Season with salt and pepper. If using immediately, keep the mushrooms warm. If using later, let the mushrooms cool completely, then cover and refrigerate for up to 1 week.

5. Preheat a grill to medium-high.

6. Grill the burgers, turning frequently, for about 8 minutes, for medium doneness. Do not press down on the burgers while they are cooking or you will squeeze out vital juices.

7. Toast the hamburger buns on the grill. Place each burger on the bottom half of a bun and top burgers with Umami Mushrooms and a Parmesan Crisp. Garnish each burger with Truffle Mayonnaise and Quick Pickled Shallots. Serve immediately.

QUINOA SUPER-STAR VEGGIE BURGER

MAKES 4 TO 6 BURGERS · REQUIRES TIME FOR PREP

We call this burger a "super-star" because it delivers! The first trick is to slightly overcook the quinoa so it is sticky and binds the burger, combine it with some of our favourite veggies and spices, and we have ourselves a winner. Another trick is to bake the burgers before frying them. This allows the burgers to set up and remain intact during the frying. Try these topped with Thai Chili Mayonnaise (page 248).

1. In a large bowl, combine the quinoa, chickpeas, black beans, green onions, spinach, mushrooms, lemon zest, ginger, salt, coriander, cumin, paprika, cayenne, eggs, and panko crumbs; mix well. Transfer the mixture to a food processor and pulse until coarsely ground. You want a mixture that is wet enough to hold together when pressed into a ball but still coarse enough that you can identify each ingredient.

2. Divide the burger mix into 4 to 6 equal portions, depending on how big you like your burger, and shape into patties. To make sure they are solid, slap the patties back and forth between your hands a couple of times. Place on a baking sheet lined with parchment paper and refrigerate for 1 or 2 hours.

3. Preheat the oven to 350°F (180°C).

4. Bake the burgers on the lined baking sheet for 20 minutes. Let cool completely, about 1 hour.

5. Once the burgers have cooled, heat the canola oil in a medium skillet over medium-high heat. Cook the burgers, carefully turning a few times, for about 8 minutes, or until they are golden, crisp, and hot. Do not press down on the burgers while they are cooking or you will break them. When done, set aside on a plate.

6. Toast the hamburger buns in the hot skillet. Place each burger on the bottom half of a bun and garnish the burgers with fresh tomato slices, greens, Quick Pickled Cucumber, and Tzatziki Sauce. Serve immediately.

2½ cups (625 mL) cooked white quinoa
¼ cup (60 mL) canned chickpeas, rinsed
¼ cup (60 mL) canned black beans, rinsed
¼ cup (60 mL) minced green onions
1 cup (250 mL) loosely packed chopped fresh baby spinach
1 cup (250 mL) finely chopped shiitake mushrooms
Grated zest of 1 lemon
1½ teaspoons (7 mL) minced fresh ginger
1½ teaspoons (7 mL) kosher salt
½ teaspoon (2 mL) ground coriander
½ teaspoon (2 mL) ground cumin
½ teaspoon (2 mL) smoked paprika
¼ teaspoon (1 mL) cayenne pepper
2 eggs, beaten
⅓ cup (75 mL) panko crumbs
⅓ cup (75 mL) canola oil
4 to 6 hamburger buns, buttered

Garnishes
Sliced tomato
Sprouts, herbs, or baby arugula
Quick Pickled Cucumber (page 254) or store-bought
Tzatziki Sauce (page 258) or store-bought

LAMB BURGER

Lamb has an amazing flavour that is both exotic and comforting all at once, which makes this not your average burger. And we've worked in the authentic Greek accompaniments in a novel way. Shown here are five sliders, which is another fun way to serve any of our burgers. Be sure to buy good-quality ground lamb, or buy a portion of shoulder or boneless neck meat and mince it up at home with the grinder attachment for your stand mixer. In the spring, we like to serve this burger with a side of Asparagus with Green Goddess Dressing (page 276).

Tomato Confit

6 ripe Roma tomatoes, peeled

2 cups (500 mL) olive oil

3 cloves garlic, peeled

5 fresh basil leaves

1 bay leaf

½ teaspoon (2 mL) kosher salt

Lamb Burgers

3 pounds (1.35 kg) ground lamb shoulder

¾ cup (175 mL) puréed white onion (about
   1 medium onion)

1 tablespoon (15 mL) kosher salt

1 teaspoon (5 mL) ground cumin

1 teaspoon (5 mL) prepared horseradish

1 teaspoon (5 mL) Worcestershire sauce

8 hamburger buns, buttered

Garnishes

1 cup (250 mL) crumbled goat feta cheese

1 cup (250 mL) Saffron Mayonnaise
   (page 248)

½ cup (125 mL) Tomato Confit
   (recipe above)

8 fresh basil leaves, for garnish

1. To make the Tomato Confit, combine the tomatoes, olive oil, garlic, basil, bay leaf, and salt in a medium saucepan. The olive oil should cover the tomatoes. Over medium heat, bring the oil to just a hint of a simmer. Cover, reduce heat, and poach for 2 hours. Check once in a while to make sure the oil is not simmering. Remove from the heat and let cool.

2. Remove the tomatoes from the olive oil. Cut them in half and remove and discard the seeds. Cut the tomatoes into strips and return them to the olive oil mixture. Store in an airtight container, refrigerated, for up to 2 weeks.

3. To make the Lamb Burgers, in a medium bowl, combine the lamb, onion purée, salt, cumin, horseradish, and Worcestershire. Mix well but without overworking (this would make the burger tough and dry). Divide the burger mix into 8 equal portions and shape into patties. To make sure they are solid but not overworked, slap the patties back and forth between your hands a couple of times. Place the burgers on a parchment-lined plate and refrigerate, covered, for 1 to 2 hours.

4. Preheat a grill to medium-high.

5. Grill the burgers, turning frequently, for about 8 minutes for medium doneness. Do not press down on the burgers while they are cooking or you will squeeze out vital juices.

6. Toast the hamburger buns on the grill. Place each burger on the bottom half of a bun and top each burger with feta cheese, Saffron Mayonnaise, Tomato Confit, and basil.

PORCHETTA SANDWICH

MAKES 4 SANDWICHES • REQUIRES TIME FOR PREP

This is quite possibly the best sandwich we serve at Bread Bar. It may seem like way too much work for a sandwich, but this is not just a sandwich—it is an experience. We use the pork shoulder, a very flavourful cut that benefits from brining, which seasons the meat throughout and keeps it moist.

The amount of roast pork in this recipe is much more than you need to make four sandwiches. Leftover pork can be covered and refrigerated for up to one week. It would be tasty chopped up in a stir-fry or with roast potatoes in a morning hash.

1. Place the pork shoulder in a large freezer bag and add the Master Brine. Seal the bag, pressing out as much air as possible to ensure all the meat is in contact with the brine. Refrigerate for 2 days.

2. Preheat the oven to 400°F (200°C).

3. Remove the pork from the brine and discard the brine. Place the pork and onion in a roasting pan and roast for 30 minutes, or until the pork has started to brown. Cover the pork with a double layer of foil, reduce the heat to 325°F (160°C), and continue to roast for a further 4 hours or until the internal temperature is 180°F (82°C). Remove the pork from the oven and baste the meat with the fat in the pan. Let the meat rest for at least 20 minutes before slicing as thinly as possible.

4. To assemble the sandwiches, pile the sliced pork on the bottom half of each bun, and season with salt and pepper. Top with Parmesan, Truffle Mayonnaise, and JC's Hot Sauce. Finish with either Salsa Rosa or Salsa Verde, if using. Add the top half of each bun, cut the sandwiches into halves or quarters, and serve immediately.

3 pounds (1.35 kg) boneless pork shoulder
1 batch Master Brine (page 250)
1 white onion, cut into quarters
4 firm ciabatta buns, cut in half and buttered
Kosher salt and freshly ground pepper
1 cup (250 mL) grated Parmesan cheese
3 tablespoons (45 mL) Truffle Mayonnaise (page 249)
2 tablespoons (30 mL) JC's Hot Sauce (page 263)
3 tablespoons (45 mL) Salsa Rosa (page 257) or Salsa Verde (page 257), optional

MARINATED CHICKPEA SANDWICH WITH ROMESCO SAUCE

MAKES 4 SANDWICHES · REQUIRES TIME FOR PREP

It is tough to dream up interesting vegetarian sandwiches. One day while Jeff was making hummus, a baker started to make a sandwich with his prep ingredients—and this sandwich was born. Regulars love this bright and flavourful vegetarian sandwich. The tang of the lemon juice is a perfect complement to the earthy chickpeas and smoky Romesco Sauce. This chickpea filling is versatile: simply add it to a cold pasta salad, serve as a side for the Piri Piri Baby Back Ribs (page 176), or make some great crostini for parties, as shown.

1. In a food processor, pulse the chickpeas three or four times, until chunky. In a medium bowl, combine the chickpeas, onion, cucumber, celery, carrot, red peppers, garlic, parsley, thyme, chili flakes, olive oil, and lemon zest and juice. Stir well. Season with salt and pepper, and adjust seasoning and spice level to taste. Cover and let marinate for 2 hours in the refrigerator.

2. To assemble the sandwiches, evenly spread the chickpea mixture over 4 toasted focaccia slices. Top each with a dollop of Romesco Sauce and garnish with arugula. Top with the remaining 4 slices of bread, cut the sandwiches in half, and serve immediately.

3 cups (750 mL) canned chickpeas, rinsed
¼ cup (60 mL) minced white onion
¼ cup (60 mL) peeled, seeded, and minced cucumber
¼ cup (60 mL) minced celery
¼ cup (60 mL) peeled and minced carrot
¼ cup (60 mL) minced roasted sweet red peppers
2 cloves garlic, minced
3 tablespoons (45 mL) minced fresh flat-leaf parsley
1 tablespoon (15 mL) minced fresh thyme
½ teaspoon (2 mL) red chili flakes
2 tablespoons (30 mL) extra-virgin olive oil
Grated zest and juice of 1 lemon
Kosher salt and freshly ground pepper
8 slices Rosemary Focaccia (page 22) or store-bought, toasted
¼ cup (60 mL) Romesco Sauce (page 260)
Arugula, for garnish

JAPANESE TUNA SALAD SANDWICH

This tuna salad can take two forms. If you use fresh tuna, then you have a very fancy tuna tartar. If you use canned tuna, then, as pictured here, you have a delicious tuna salad sandwich. The miso paste adds an exotic flavour that our customers love. Tuna is overfished in many parts of the world, so be careful when at the market. Ask for fish sourced in a responsible and sustainable way. This salad is also delicious as a topping on steamed rice.

2 cans (5 ounces/142 g each) albacore tuna in water (or ½ pound/225 g fresh tuna)

1 clove garlic, chopped

1 teaspoon (5 mL) pine nuts, chopped

1 teaspoon (5 mL) chopped fresh dill

1 teaspoon (5 mL) chopped fresh basil

1 teaspoon (5 mL) raw sunflower seeds

1 tablespoon (15 mL) light (sweet) miso paste

1 tablespoon (15 mL) unseasoned rice vinegar

2 teaspoons (10 mL) lightly packed brown sugar

1 teaspoon (5 mL) soy sauce

¼ teaspoon (1 mL) sesame oil

¼ cup (60 mL) Basic Mayonnaise (page 246) or store-bought

8 slices crusty sourdough bread, toasted and buttered

1. Drain the canned tuna. If using fresh tuna, finely dice it.

2. In a medium bowl, combine the tuna with the garlic, pine nuts, dill, basil, sunflower seeds, miso paste, rice vinegar, brown sugar, soy sauce, sesame oil, and Basic Mayonnaise; mix well.

3. Evenly divide the tuna mixture among 4 slices of buttered toast and gently mash and spread with a fork. Top with the remaining 4 slices of toast, cut the sandwiches into halves or quarters, and serve immediately.

AVOCADO, TOMATO, CHICKEN, AND BACON SANDWICH

This is our most popular sandwich at Bread Bar. We are not sure if that's because of the bacon or the avocado. Either way it is a winner, and every summer we look forward to its return to the menu. You can tell when an avocado is ripe by its colour and feel: it should be dark, not light green, and when you gently squeeze it, it should yield slightly. We often pair this sandwich with the Arugula and Fennel Salad (page 49).

3 boneless, skinless chicken breasts

1 lemon, quartered

Kosher salt and freshly ground pepper

12 slices bacon

8 slices sandwich bread

Good-quality salted butter

1 ripe avocado, pitted, peeled, and sliced

2 medium ripe tomatoes, sliced

¼ cup (60 mL) Chipotle Mayonnaise (page 246)

1. Preheat the oven to 350°F (180°C). Line a baking sheet with parchment paper.

2. Place the chicken breasts on the baking sheet, squeeze the lemon over them, and drop the lemon quarters on the tray. Season with salt and pepper. Roast the chicken with the lemon for 30 minutes, or until the internal temperature reaches 160°F (70°C). Discard the lemon and let the chicken cool. When cool, slice the chicken as thickly or thinly as you like.

3. In a medium skillet over medium-high heat, cook the bacon until golden brown and crisp. Transfer to paper towels to drain.

4. Butter the bread. Evenly arrange the chicken, bacon, avocado, and tomato on 4 slices of bread. Season with salt and pepper, and drizzle with Chipotle Mayonnaise. Top with the remaining 4 slices of bread, cut the sandwiches into halves or quarters, and serve.

CRISPY EGGPLANT MELT

MAKES 4 SANDWICHES

Having a mouthful of this sandwich should be on your bucket list. Eggplant Parmesan is a traditional Italian side dish, but as a sandwich it's a real game changer. Choose a glossy, plump eggplant that feels heavy in your hand. Since this sandwich is a summer menu item, we suggest you serve it with Heirloom Tomato Salad (page 58) on the side.

---

1. Place the flour in a medium bowl. Beat the eggs in a second medium bowl. Place the panko crumbs in a shallow dish.

2. Cut the eggplant crosswise into 1-inch (2.5 cm) slices. Dredge the eggplant slices in the flour, shaking off excess, and place on a baking sheet. Working with one slice at a time, dip the eggplant slices into the egg to coat, then dip them into the panko crumbs, pressing firmly and covering all the surfaces. Set aside on the baking sheet.

3. Preheat the oven to 350°F (180°C). Line a baking sheet with parchment paper.

4. Heat the olive oil in a large skillet over medium-high heat. Working in batches if necessary, carefully add the breaded eggplant. Fry for 3 minutes per side, or until golden brown and crisp on both sides. Transfer as cooked to the baking sheet.

5. Evenly top the eggplant slices with Red Sauce, then top with mozzarella cheese. Bake until the eggplant is hot and the cheese has fully melted, about 10 minutes.

6. To assemble the sandwiches, place the hot eggplant on the bottom half of each bun. Season with salt and pepper, and garnish with fresh basil and chili flakes. Add the top of each bun, cut the sandwiches into halves or quarters, and serve.

3 tablespoons (45 mL) all-purpose flour
3 large eggs
4 cups (1 L) panko crumbs
1 large Italian eggplant
1 cup (250 mL) olive oil
2 cups (500 mL) Red Sauce (page 259)
2 cups (500 mL) shredded mozzarella cheese
4 Italian buns, cut in half
Kosher salt and freshly ground pepper
8 fresh basil leaves, for garnish
1 teaspoon (5 mL) red chili flakes, for garnish

FRIED CHICKEN SANDWICH

MAKES 4 SANDWICHES · REQUIRES TIME FOR PREP

This incredible fried chicken sandwich is so popular at Bread Bar that it sells out most days we offer it on the menu. Brining the chicken is key to its firm texture and moistness after frying. This sandwich goes well with Peach and Mozzarella Salad (page 68).

4 skinless, boneless chicken thighs
1 batch Master Brine (page 250)
1½ cups (375 mL) all-purpose flour
½ cup (125 mL) potato starch or cornstarch
2 tablespoons (30 mL) salt
1 tablespoon (15 mL) garlic powder
1 tablespoon (15 mL) onion powder
1 tablespoon (15 mL) hot paprika
1 teaspoon (5 mL) cayenne pepper
2 cups (500 mL) buttermilk
Canola oil, for frying
4 hamburger buns, buttered

Garnishes
4 ounces (115 g) blue cheese, crumbled
2 tablespoons (30 mL) Basic Mayonnaise
   (page 246) or store-bought
2 tablespoons (30 mL) JC's Hot Sauce
   (page 263)
2 dill pickles, cut in half lengthwise

1. Place the chicken thighs in a large resealable freezer bag and add the Master Brine. Seal the bag, pressing out as much air as possible to ensure all the chicken is in contact with the brine. Refrigerate for 24 hours.

2. In a large bowl, combine the flour, potato starch, salt, garlic powder, onion powder, paprika, and cayenne. Pour the buttermilk into a separate large bowl.

3. Drain the chicken and discard the brine. Add the chicken to the buttermilk, turning to completely coat. Then, working with one piece at a time, dredge the chicken in the flour mixture, pressing and turning so the flour sticks to all sides. If you like a thick crust, repeat the process with each piece of chicken, starting in the buttermilk. Place the chicken on a plate and chill for 1 hour.

4. Fit a large, heavy pot with a deep-fat thermometer and pour in enough canola oil to come halfway up the sides. Heat the oil over medium-high to 350°F (180°C). Carefully add the chicken and fry, turning often and adjusting the heat to maintain the temperature, until deep golden brown and the internal temperature is 160°F (70°C), about 8 minutes. Transfer the chicken to paper towels to drain.

5. Toast the hamburger buns in a large skillet or under the broiler. Place a chicken thigh on the bottom half of each bun and garnish with blue cheese, Basic Mayonnaise, JC's Hot Sauce, and a pickle half. Serve immediately.

PEAR AND PROSCIUTTO SANDWICH

MAKES 4 SANDWICHES

We love prosciutto—you can taste all the time it took hanging in the Italian air, slowly curing, becoming something much more than just a ham. When we combine prosciutto, pears, and Brie, these ingredients create fantastic flavours, fresh and earthy all at once. We often serve this sandwich with the Squash and Apple Salad (page 53).

1. Butter the baguette halves. Evenly arrange the pear slices, Brie, and prosciutto on the bottom half of each baguette. Top with the watercress, season with salt and pepper, and drizzle the honey on top. Add the top halves of each loaf, cut the sandwiches into halves or quarters, and serve.

2 baguettes, sliced horizontally

4 tablespoons (60 mL) high-quality salted butter, softened

2 Bartlett pears, cored and thinly sliced

4 ounces (115 g) Brie, cut into eight ½-inch (1 cm) slices

8 thin slices prosciutto

1 bunch watercress, trimmed

Kosher salt and freshly ground pepper

2 tablespoons (30 mL) liquid honey (we use local blueberry honey)

TOMATO, GOAT CHEESE, AND CARAMELIZED ONION TARTINE

The flavour combination of tomato, goat cheese, and caramelized onion dates back a long way, to when we were young, hungry cooks trying to figure this all out. We served these small tartines at one of our first catering gigs, and it was the first time someone proclaimed our food delicious. What more can young cooks ask for! This tartine pairs well with our Arugula and Fennel Salad (page 49).

4 thick slices Rosemary Focaccia
(page 22) or store-bought
4 tablespoons (60 mL) extra-virgin olive
oil, divided
24 ripe cherry tomatoes
Kosher salt and freshly ground pepper
½ cup (125 mL) soft goat cheese
1 cup (250 mL) Caramelized Onions
(page 250)
¼ cup (60 mL) House Vinaigrette
(page 244)
1 tablespoon (15 mL) chopped fresh thyme
1 lemon

1. Set an oven rack at the highest level and preheat the broiler.

2. Brush one side of the bread with 2 tablespoons (30 mL) of the olive oil and place on one side of a baking sheet.

3. In a medium bowl, toss the cherry tomatoes with the remaining 2 tablespoons (30 mL) olive oil and season with salt. Place the tomatoes on the baking sheet next to the bread.

4. Place the baking sheet under the broiler on the highest rack and broil until the bread is toasted on one side and the tomatoes are blistered. Watch carefully, as they may be done at different times.

5. Spread the goat cheese evenly over each slice of toasted focaccia. Top with the Caramelized Onions. Divide the tomatoes among the slices. Drizzle with the House Vinaigrette and sprinkle with fresh thyme and a squeeze of lemon juice. Season with salt and pepper. Serve immediately.

PIZZAS

NANCY SILVERTON

PIZZERIA MOZZA, LOS ANGELES, CALIFORNIA

Nancy Silverton has had an amazing career with a few hiccups along the way, but who hasn't encountered an obstacle or two en route to success? After studying at Le Cordon Bleu in London and École Lenôtre in France (Nancy and Bettina both studied political science in university and then went on to study pastry at École Lenôtre), Silverton was hired by Wolfgang Puck to be the pastry chef for Spago, in Los Angeles, when it opened in 1982. Then, in 1986, she wrote her first cookbook, *Desserts*. In 1989 in she opened Campanile and La Brea Bakery with her husband at the time, chef Mark Peel. La Brea Bakery functioned as a bakery attached to the restaurant. Sound familiar?

Silverton mixed, shaped, and baked every single loaf herself, and La Brea was so successful—they would sell out of bread by lunchtime—that they had to expand. Yet once industrial-size machines and mechanized production lines took over, Silverton no longer had hands-on control over the baking process. That was difficult for her—a dilemma that Jeff appreciates. For years he mixed and shaped by hand every loaf of bread and every pizza dough. Using production equipment seemed so counterintuitive that initially he resisted at Bread Bar. In the end,

though, these tools were so helpful, he cannot imagine doing without them now. But to hand off all production control is another thing altogether, and in 2001 Silverton made the tough decision to sell La Brea.

In 2007, she opened Pizzeria Mozza—to immediate critical acclaim. This restaurant above all others was a direct inspiration for Bread Bar. Jeff loves to explore the practices of successful restaurants, so, true to form, he went to Pizzeria Mozza on a reconnaissance mission. Mozza was of interest because it was similar to the place we intended to open and provided an experience like the one we wanted our customers to have. Mozza turned out to be a bright, airy space with zero pretension, but it clearly took its food and hospitality seriously. (Again, sound familiar?) Jeff returned from California with a new attitude toward restaurants. Previously food focused, Jeff conceded that a restaurant's success is dependent on creating an overall experience for guests. And, that food was a small portion of the complete dining experience.

A great restaurant doesn't just serve great food. It makes you feel special. That was the lightning in a bottle he wanted to capture in Bread Bar.

When we began to think about how to serve hundreds of pizzas at Bread Bar, the key question was how do we cook hundreds of litres of tomato sauce? Jeff's visit to Mozza provided the answer. You don't cook it—the sauce cooks on the pizza! Brilliant. Lesson learned. (Check out our Red Sauce on page 259.) Question two: How does Mozza get those amazing blackened, blistered bubbles on the crust? Answer: They hand-stretch every pizza with a very specific technique. We copied this technique outright with excellent results, and we teach it to everyone who has time to hand-roll dough—including service staff. If we can get a bunch of pizza dough rolled out throughout the day, lunch and dinner service are so much smoother.

And finally there was the question of Mozza's pizza dough—what were the secrets to its success? Nancy Silverton spent a lot of time perfecting her dough. She describes bread as being alive, something that can't be controlled. You must guide and continually tweak it. Given that Mozza and Bread Bar exist in different environments, and we each use different flours, our dough is very specific to Bread Bar. It took a few months of experimentation before we opened, but we did develop a pizza dough for our climate, service, and customers.

After Jeff introduced her to Silverton's work, Bettina realized how similar her approach to food is to Silverton's—they even have the same thoughts about bread. Bread is a living thing that demands your patience and presence. Every aspect of its formation is nurtured and coaxed into being. And the process is never finished, for the recipe is constantly being tweaked to accommodate minor changes in ingredients and environment. Call bread baking high-maintenance if you will, but it's also expressive and comforting—there's nothing quite like it.

Silverton's food is connected to the land, expressive and comforting like a Sunday dinner. Her dishes seem familiar at first but are flavourful in a distinct and memorable way. This is exactly what we serve at Bread Bar, dishes such as macaroni and cheese, salads, burgers, pizza, and desserts from our childhood memories.

When Mozza opened, Silverton sent a shock wave of flavour through the Los Angeles dining community, and we like to think that we did the same with Bread Bar, at least in our neighbourhood. We work very hard to make our food delicious, and we have Nancy Silverton to thank for inspiring what Bread Bar has become today.

1. In a small bowl, combine the water, olive oil, and yeast. In a large bowl, combine the flour and salt. Add the wet ingredients to the dry ingredients and mix well until the flour is incorporated and a dough forms, about 5 minutes. The dough may look a little rough and shaggy—that's fine. Cover the bowl with plastic wrap and let rise in the fridge for 24 hours. The dough should double in size. (This cool, slow rise is where the magic happens. The dough will be easier to stretch and the pizza will have a crisper crust and more flavour.)

2. Flour a work surface, scrape the dough onto it, and dust generously with flour. Divide the dough into 4 equal parts. If the dough still feels slightly sticky, dust it with more flour.

3. Spray four 3-inch (8 cm) round plastic containers (such as sour cream containers, washed and dried) with non-stick cooking spray and place a dough portion in each container. Cover and let the dough rest at room temperature for about an hour. (If you don't intend to use the dough right away, the balls can be refrigerated for up to 2 days or frozen for up to a month.)

4. To shape the dough into rounds, generously flour a work surface. Tip 1 ball of dough onto the floured surface and dust the top with more flour. Starting from the inside and working your way out, press down and gently stretch the dough out to about 7 inches (18 cm). Carefully continue this process, massaging the dough into a disc about 10 inches (25 cm) across. Be careful not to press down on the edges (this will be your amazing crust). If gas bubbles appear, this is a good sign—leave them alone.

PIZZA DOUGH

MAKES 4 BALLS OF PIZZA DOUGH, ENOUGH FOR FOUR 10-INCH (25 CM) PIZZAS • REQUIRES TIME FOR PREP

Being pizza lovers, we have great respect for the dough and the crust. We have developed this recipe to give you a reliable high-quality dough to make at home. With this recipe, you will be able to turn out a delicious pizza with an amazing crust, every time.

Just like bread dough, pizza dough is unpredictable. Flour, humidity, yeast, and temperature all affect fermentation time. The good news is that practice makes perfect. If you are not used to handling pizza dough, have no fear—anyone can make a great crust. Just be sure to make the dough two days before you intend to make the pizza, giving the dough plenty of time to develop flavour.

Your oven needs to be as hot as possible. Preheat for at least half an hour. At Bread Bar, we use an oven with a stone deck, which you can recreate at home with a pizza stone. The porous nature of stone absorbs moisture from the dough, resulting in a crisper crust. You can always use a baking sheet instead, but pizza stones are inexpensive and make all the difference, so we recommend purchasing one.

2 cups + 1 tablespoon (515 mL) warm water
2 tablespoons (30 mL) extra-virgin olive oil
1½ teaspoons (7 mL) instant dry yeast
4 cups (1 L) unbleached organic bread flour
1 tablespoon (15 mL) kosher salt
Special equipment: four 3-inch (8 cm) plastic containers

MARGHERITA PIZZA

MAKES ONE 10-INCH (25 CM) PIZZA

There are many different styles of pizza in the world. We consider ours to be "neo-Neapolitan." At Bread Bar, we cook our pizzas at 600°F (315°C) rather than the 900°F (480°C) an authentic Neapolitan style requires. We prefer the crust to be crispy, and cooking at 900°F (480 ˚C) tends to leave the crust too soft for our taste. Cooking at a lower heat, we can't put fresh mozzarella cheese on our Margherita Pizza, since it would melt into a milky liquid during the comparatively long cooking time (true Neapolitan pizza cooks in 90 seconds). So instead we use an aged low-moisture mozzarella cut into 1-inch (2.5 cm) cubes that can handle the time in the oven. Pair this pizza with the Chopped Salad (page 61) or the Tuscan Kale and Bread Soup (page 33).

---

1 ball pizza dough, shaped as directed on page 139

½ cup (125 mL) Red Sauce (page 259)

¼ cup (60 mL) shredded mozzarella cheese

4 cubes (1 inch/2.5 cm each) full-fat low-moisture mozzarella cheese (we use local Salerno)

2 cloves garlic, minced

8 fresh basil leaves, divided

1 tablespoon (15 mL) extra-virgin olive oil, for garnish

½ teaspoon (2 mL) coarse sea salt, for garnish

1. Place a pizza stone on the top shelf of the oven and preheat to 550°F (290°C) or the highest setting. Let the stone heat for an additional 30 minutes after the oven has reached its set temperature. (If you don't have a pizza stone, you can use a rimless baking sheet.)

2. Generously flour a pizza peel or rimless baking sheet. Transfer the stretched dough to the peel or tray and give it a shake to ensure the dough is not sticking to it. Evenly spread the Red Sauce over the pizza dough, stopping about 1 inch (2.5 cm) from the edge. Scatter the shredded mozzarella evenly over the sauce, then top with the cubed mozzarella, garlic, and 4 basil leaves.

3. To transfer the pizza to the stone, place the peel over the stone and quickly pull the peel back towards you. (Or lift out the hot baking sheet, slide the pizza onto it, and return to the oven.) Bake for 9 minutes (or 11 minutes if baking on a baking sheet), or until the edges are slightly charred and crispy. Keep a close eye on it.

4. Use the pizza peel to remove the pizza to a cutting board. Garnish with the remaining 4 basil leaves, the olive oil, and salt. Slice and serve immediately.

APPLE BACON PIZZA

This is our bestselling pizza. Autumn inspired the toppings, and the combination of tart, rich, and smoky hit the nail on the head! This pizza will be on our menu until the end of time. It goes well with the Cauliflower Soup (page 37).

1. Place a pizza stone on the top shelf of the oven and preheat to 550°F (290°C) or the highest setting. Let the stone heat for an additional 30 minutes after the oven has reached its set temperature. (If you don't have a pizza stone, you can use a rimless baking sheet.)

2. Generously flour a pizza peel or rimless baking sheet. Transfer the stretched dough to the peel or tray and give it a shake to ensure the dough is not sticking to it. Evenly spread the White Sauce over the pizza dough, stopping about 1 inch (2.5 cm) from the edge. Scatter the mozzarella evenly over the sauce, then top with the Caramelized Onions, thyme, bacon, and apple slices.

3. To transfer the pizza to the stone, place the peel over the stone and quickly pull the peel back towards you. (Or lift out the hot baking sheet, slide the pizza onto it, and return to the oven.) Bake for 9 minutes (or 11 minutes if baking on a baking sheet), or until the edges are slightly charred and crispy. Keep a close eye on it.

4. Use the pizza peel to remove the pizza to a cutting board. Garnish with the smoked cheddar and sage leaves. Slice and serve immediately.

1 ball pizza dough, shaped as directed on page 139

½ cup (125 mL) White Sauce (page 259)

1 cup (250 mL) shredded mozzarella cheese

2 tablespoons (30 mL) Caramelized Onions (page 250)

1 teaspoon (5 mL) chopped fresh thyme

3 strips (3 ounces/85 g) bacon, cooked and cut into 1-inch (2.5 cm) chunks (about ¼ cup/60 mL)

½ apple, cored and thinly sliced (we use Golden Delicious)

¼ cup (60 mL) grated smoked cheddar cheese, for garnish

5 fresh sage leaves, for garnish

GOAT CHEESE AND BACON PIZZA

MAKES ONE 10-INCH (25 CM) PIZZA

To make a truly incredible pizza, you need to put some love and care into every detail. Good ingredients matter, and really do make a difference. For this recipe, shop for the best goat cheese you can afford and a nice thick piece of double-smoked bacon. We often pair this pizza with the Chopped Salad (page 61).

1 ball pizza dough, shaped as directed on page 139

½ cup (125 mL) Red Sauce (page 259)

1 cup (250 mL) shredded mozzarella cheese

1 clove garlic, minced

3 strips (3 ounces/85 g) bacon, cooked and cut into 1-inch (2.5 cm) chunks (about ½ cup/125 mL)

¼ cup (60 mL) soft goat cheese, plus more for garnish

½ cup (125 mL) thinly sliced green onions, plus more for garnish

1. Place a pizza stone on the top shelf of the oven and preheat to 550°F (290°C) or the highest setting. Let the stone heat for an additional 30 minutes after the oven has reached its set temperature. (If you don't have a pizza stone, you can use a rimless baking sheet.)

2. Generously flour a pizza peel or rimless baking sheet. Transfer the stretched dough to the peel or tray and give it a shake to ensure the dough is not sticking to it. Evenly spread the Red Sauce over the pizza dough, stopping about 1 inch (2.5 cm) from the edge. Scatter the mozzarella over the sauce, then top with the garlic, bacon, goat cheese, and green onions.

3. To transfer the pizza to the stone, place the peel over the stone and quickly pull the peel back towards you. (Or lift out the hot baking sheet, slide the pizza onto it, and return to the oven.) Bake for 9 minutes (or 11 minutes if baking on a baking sheet), or until the edges are slightly charred and crispy. Keep a close eye on it.

4. Use the pizza peel to remove the pizza to a cutting board. Garnish with a little more goat cheese and green onions. Slice and serve immediately.

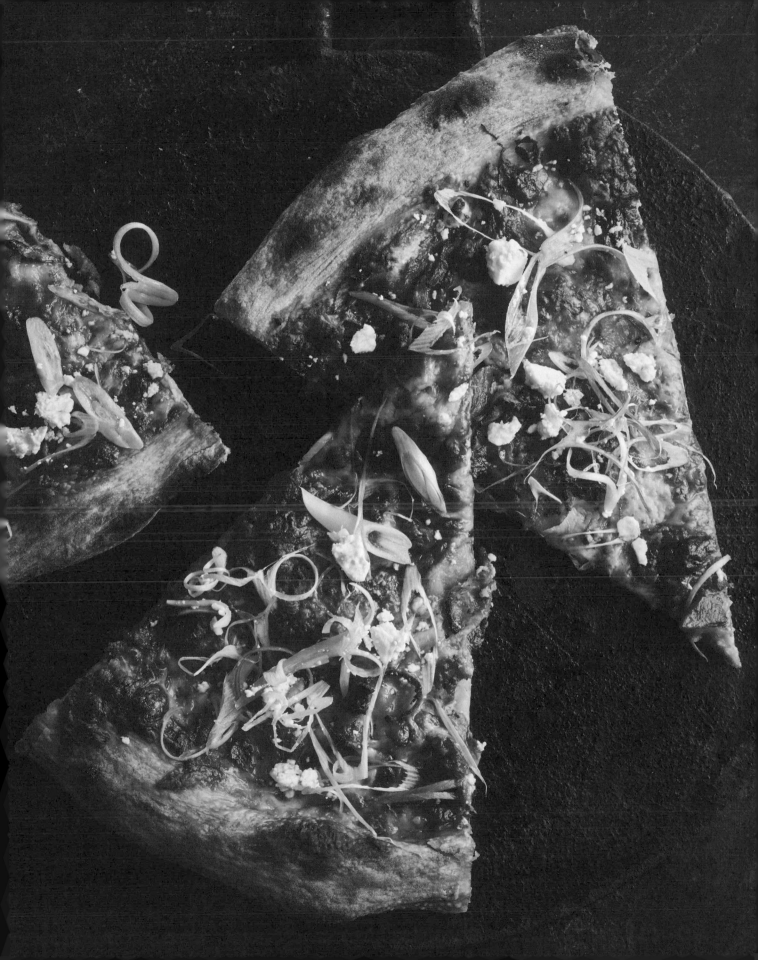

BEE STING PIZZA

MAKES ONE 10-INCH (25 CM) PIZZA

The Bee Sting is inspired by one of our favourite pizza joints in the world, Roberta's, in Bushwick, New York. The bite of the spicy salami, the sweet honey, and the soft cheese is a combination worth travelling for—except now you don't have to! Use the spiciest salami you can find for a truly fantastic pizza. This pairs well with Grilled Octopus with Potatoes and Mint (page 86). (Shown on opposite page, left side of pizza.)

1. Place a pizza stone on the top shelf of the oven and preheat to 550°F (290°C) or the highest setting. Let the stone heat for an additional 30 minutes after the oven has reached its set temperature. (If you don't have a pizza stone, you can use a rimless baking sheet.)

2. Generously flour a pizza peel or rimless baking sheet. Transfer the stretched dough to the peel or tray and give it a shake to ensure the dough is not sticking to it. Evenly spread the Red Sauce over the pizza dough, stopping about 1 inch (2.5 cm) from the edge. Scatter the mozzarella evenly over the sauce, then top with the salami, ricotta, and chilies.

3. To transfer the pizza to the stone, place the peel over the stone and quickly pull the peel back towards you. (Or lift out the hot baking sheet, slide the pizza onto it, and return to the oven.) Bake for 9 minutes (or 11 minutes if baking on a baking sheet), or until the edges are slightly charred and crispy. Keep a close eye on it.

4. Use the pizza peel to remove the pizza to a cutting board. Garnish with the basil and drizzle over the honey. Slice and serve immediately.

1 ball pizza dough, shaped as directed on page 139
½ cup (125 mL) Red Sauce (page 259)
1 cup (250 mL) shredded mozzarella cheese
6 thin slices spicy salami
½ cup (125 mL) ricotta cheese, drained well
¼ cup (60 mL) sliced long red chili, seeded
5 fresh basil leaves, for garnish
2 tablespoons (30 mL) liquid honey, for garnish

BUTTER CHICKEN PIZZA

MAKES ONE 10-INCH (25 CM) PIZZA

We like to have fun with our pizza toppings. When one of our cooks made a butter chicken pizza, we were skeptical. We thought it was just an over-the-top play on Indian food, but were we wrong! This pizza stands up to the authenticity test. After all, our pizza dough is very close to naan bread, a traditional accompaniment to curries. Share this pizza with the Spicy Lentil, Wild Rice, and Orzo Salad (page 71) or Curried Lentil Soup with Coconut Yogurt (page 36). (Shown on page 146, right side of pizza.)

1 ball pizza dough, shaped as directed on page 139

½ cup (125 mL) Butter Chicken Sauce (page 261)

½ cup (125 mL) shredded mozzarella cheese

3 ounces (85 g) cooked chicken breast, thinly sliced

1 cup (250 mL) thinly sliced red onion

¼ cup (60 mL) sliced long red chili, seeded

1 tablespoon (15 mL) chopped fresh cilantro, for garnish

1 teaspoon (5 mL) grated lime zest, for garnish

3 tablespoons (45 mL) plain full-fat yogurt, for garnish

1. Place a pizza stone on the top shelf of the oven and preheat to 550°F (290°C) or the highest setting. Let the stone heat for an additional 30 minutes after the oven has reached its set temperature. (If you don't have a pizza stone, you can use a rimless baking sheet.)

2. Generously flour a pizza peel or rimless baking sheet. Transfer the stretched dough to the peel or tray and give it a shake to ensure the dough is not sticking to it. Evenly spread the Butter Chicken Sauce over the pizza dough, stopping about 1 inch (2.5 cm) from the edge. Scatter the mozzarella evenly over the sauce, then top with the chicken, red onion, and chilies.

3. To transfer the pizza to the stone, place the peel over the stone and quickly pull the peel back towards you. (Or lift out the hot baking sheet, slide the pizza onto it, and return to the oven.) Bake for 9 minutes (or 11 minutes if baking on a baking sheet), or until the edges are slightly charred and crispy. Keep a close eye on it.

4. Use the pizza peel to remove the pizza to a cutting board. Garnish with the cilantro and lime zest and drizzle over the yogurt. Slice and serve immediately.

GREEN GODDESS PIZZA

MAKES ONE 10-INCH (25 CM) PIZZA

Many of our customers are vegetarians, so we take special care to create pizzas for them. Veggie pizzas require some thought and care because they can fall flat in flavour due to the lack of fat content. This one tastes amazing even to carnivores like us because of the green goddess tang. Get creative with the toppings on this pizza and use any seasonal vegetables you like. (Shown on page 151, bottom pizza.)

1. Place a pizza stone on the top shelf of the oven and preheat to 550°F (290°C) or the highest setting. Let the stone heat for an additional 30 minutes after the oven has reached its set temperature. (If you don't have a pizza stone, you can use a rimless baking sheet.)

2. Generously flour a pizza peel or rimless baking sheet. Transfer the stretched dough to the peel or tray and give it a shake to ensure the dough is not sticking to it. Evenly spread the Red Sauce over the pizza dough, stopping about 1 inch (2.5 cm) from the edge. Scatter the mozzarella evenly over the sauce, then top with the kale, spinach, ricotta, asparagus, olive oil, and chilies.

3. To transfer the pizza to the stone, place the peel over the stone and quickly pull the peel back towards you. (Or lift out the hot baking sheet, slide the pizza onto it, and return to the oven.) Bake for 9 minutes (or 11 minutes if baking on a baking sheet), or until the edges are slightly charred and crispy. Keep a close eye on it.

4. Use the pizza peel to remove the pizza to a cutting board. Garnish with lemon zest and drizzle with Green Goddess Dressing. Slice and serve immediately.

1 ball pizza dough, shaped as directed on page 139
½ cup (125 mL) Red Sauce (page 259)
1 cup (250 mL) shredded mozzarella cheese
Handful of baby kale
Handful of baby spinach
½ cup (125 mL) ricotta cheese, drained well
2 spears asparagus, trimmed and sliced on the diagonal
2 tablespoons (30 mL) olive oil
¼ cup (60 mL) sliced long red chili, seeded
1½ teaspoons (7 mL) grated lemon zest, for garnish
2 tablespoons (30 mL) Green Goddess Dressing (page 244), for garnish

ROASTED MUSHROOM PIZZA

MAKES ONE 10-INCH (25 CM) PIZZA

Mushrooms are comfort food to us—warm, earthy, and meaty in their own way. Maybe we all have a bit of cream of mushroom soup nostalgia in us. Wild mushrooms like morels and chanterelles have a deeper flavour than cultivated mushrooms. They are easy to find at good produce markets, for a price. In a pinch, dried wild mushrooms, rehydrated well, are an acceptable substitute. Pair this pizza with the exotic Roasted Eggplant with Miso and Green Peppers (page 73). (Shown on opposite page, top pizza.)

Roasted Mushrooms
(makes 2 cups/ 500 mL)

3 tablespoons (45 mL) olive oil

4 cups (1 L) mixed mushrooms (button, shiitake, cremini, oyster, chanterelle), chopped

1 tablespoons (15 mL) water

2 tablespoons (30 mL) unsalted butter

1 clove garlic, minced

1 shallot, minced

1½ teaspoons (7 mL) minced fresh thyme

1½ teaspoons (7 mL) minced fresh chives

Kosher salt and freshly ground pepper

Pizza

1 ball pizza dough, shaped as directed on page 139

½ cup (125 mL) Red Sauce (page 259)

1 cup (250 mL) shredded mozzarella cheese

1 tablespoon (15 mL) grated Fontina cheese

1 teaspoon (5 mL) minced fresh thyme

1 green onion, thinly sliced, for garnish

1. To roast the mushrooms, heat the olive oil in a large skillet over high heat. Add the mushrooms and water. Cook, without stirring, for about 8 minutes. Stir, then continue to cook, stirring frequently, until the mushrooms are dry, about 4 minutes. Remove from the heat and stir in the butter, garlic, shallot, thyme, and chives. Season with salt and pepper and set aside.

2. Place a pizza stone on the top shelf of the oven and preheat to 550°F (290°C) or the highest setting. Let the stone heat for an additional 30 minutes after the oven has reached its set temperature. (If you don't have a pizza stone, you can use a rimless baking sheet.)

3. Generously flour a pizza peel or rimless baking sheet. Transfer the stretched dough to the peel or tray and give it a shake to ensure the dough is not sticking to it. Evenly spread the Red Sauce over the pizza dough, stopping about 1 inch (2.5 cm) from the edge. Scatter the mozzarella cheese evenly over the sauce, then top with 1½ cups (375 mL) of the roasted mushrooms, the Fontina, and thyme.

4. To transfer the pizza to the stone, place the peel over the stone and quickly pull the peel back towards you. (Or lift out the hot baking sheet, slide the pizza onto it, and return to the oven.) Bake for 9 minutes (or 11 minutes if baking on a baking sheet), or until the edges are slightly charred and crispy. Keep a close eye on it.

5. Use the pizza peel to remove the pizza to a cutting board. Garnish with green onions. Slice and serve immediately.

CHEESE LOUISE PIZZA

MAKES ONE 10-INCH (25 CM) PIZZA

The Cheese Louise is on fire at Bread Bar. One of our latest creations, it has struck a chord with customers and now has a loyal following. You can be creative with the types of cheese you use. We have found it is best to select a firm cheese, a soft cheese, and a pungent cheese.

---

1. Place a pizza stone on the top shelf of the oven and preheat to 550°F (290°C) or the highest setting. Let the stone heat for an additional 30 minutes after the oven has reached its set temperature. (If you don't have a pizza stone, you can use a rimless baking sheet.)

2. Generously flour a pizza peel or rimless baking sheet. Transfer the stretched dough to the peel or tray and give it a shake to ensure the dough is not sticking to it. Evenly spread the White Sauce over the pizza dough, stopping about 1 inch (2.5 cm) from the edge. Scatter the mozzarella evenly over the sauce, then top with the Taleggio, goat, and Fontina cheeses.

3. To transfer the pizza to the stone, place the peel over the stone and quickly pull the peel back towards you. (Or lift out the hot baking sheet, slide the pizza onto it, and return to the oven.) Bake for 9 minutes (or 11 minutes if baking on a baking sheet), or until the edges are slightly charred and crispy. Keep a close eye on it.

4. Use the pizza peel to remove the pizza to a cutting board. Garnish with the parsley and a drizzle of truffle honey. Slice and serve immediately.

1 ball pizza dough, shaped as directed on page 139

½ cup (125 mL) White Sauce (page 259)

¼ cup (60 mL) shredded mozzarella cheese

2 tablespoons (30 mL) sliced Taleggio cheese

2 tablespoons (30 mL) soft goat cheese

1 tablespoon (15 mL) grated Fontina cheese

1 teaspoon (5 mL) minced fresh flat-leaf parsley, for garnish

1 tablespoon (15 mL) truffle honey, for garnish

THE ROB PIZZA

At Bread Bar, we have a take-out counter for pastries and free-style pizza by the slice. When this pizza first showed up on the counter, customers noticed that one chef made it. Suddenly we had phone orders for "that pizza that Rob makes." And so The Rob Pizza was born. Pair this pizza with the Corn and Poblano Soup (page 30).

---

1 ball pizza dough, shaped as directed on page 139

½ cup (125 mL) White Sauce (page 259)

1 cup (250 mL) shredded mozzarella cheese

½ cup (125 mL) Roasted Mushrooms (page 154)

5 cloves Garlic Confit (page 253)

¼ cup (60 mL) soft goat cheese

¼ cup (60 mL) Caramelized Onions (page 250)

1 green onion, thinly sliced

1. Place a pizza stone on the top shelf of the oven and preheat to 550°F (290°C) or the highest setting. Let the stone heat for an additional 30 minutes after the oven has reached its set temperature. (If you don't have a pizza stone, you can use a rimless baking sheet.)

2. Generously flour a pizza peel or rimless baking sheet. Transfer the stretched dough to the peel or tray and give it a shake to ensure the dough is not sticking to it. Evenly spread the White Sauce over the pizza dough, stopping about 1 inch (2.5 cm) from the edge. Scatter the mozzarella evenly over the sauce, then top with Roasted Mushrooms, Garlic Confit, goat cheese, Caramelized Onions, and green onions.

3. To transfer the pizza to the stone, place the peel over the stone and quickly pull the peel back towards you. (Or lift out the hot baking sheet, slide the pizza onto it, and return to the oven.) Bake for 9 minutes (or 11 minutes if baking on a baking sheet), or until the edges are slightly charred and crispy. Keep a close eye on it.

4. Use the pizza peel to remove the pizza to a cutting board. Slice and serve immediately.

VAMPIRE SLAYER PIZZA

Dreaming up fun names for our pizza creations has a long tradition at Bread Bar. This one is inspired by Buffy. It may look like a lot of garlic, but when the cloves are slowly poached in olive oil, the astringent garlic flavour is softened. To our surprise this pizza has gained quite a following and is sorely missed when it comes off the menu each spring. It goes well with the Roasted Eggplant with Miso and Green Peppers (page 73).

1. Place a pizza stone on the top shelf of the oven and preheat to 550°F (290°C) or the highest setting. Let the stone heat for an additional 30 minutes after the oven has reached its set temperature. (If you don't have a pizza stone, you can use a rimless baking sheet.)

2. Generously flour a pizza peel or rimless baking sheet. Transfer the stretched dough to the peel or tray and give it a shake to ensure the dough is not sticking to it. Evenly spread the White Sauce over the pizza dough, stopping about 1 inch (2.5 cm) from the edge. Scatter the mozzarella evenly over the sauce, then top with the Brie slices.

3. To transfer the pizza to the stone, place the peel over the stone and quickly pull the peel back towards you. (Or lift out the hot baking sheet, slide the pizza onto it, and return to the oven.) Bake for 9 minutes (or 11 minutes if baking on a baking sheet), or until the edges are slightly charred and crispy. Keep a close eye on it

4. Use the pizza peel to remove the pizza to a cutting board. Garnish with Garlic Confit, arugula, and lemon zest. Slice and serve immediately.

1 ball pizza dough, shaped as directed on page 139
1 cup (250 mL) White Sauce (page 259)
¾ cup (175 mL) shredded mozzarella cheese
3 ounces (85 g) Brie, sliced

Garnishes
11 cloves Garlic Confit (page 253)
Handful of baby arugula
1 teaspoon (5 mL) grated lemon zest

WISE GUY PIZZA

Whenever we have a craving for spice and meat (which is often!), the Wise Guy is our cure.
It is an excellent complement to the Bee Sting Pizza (page 147).

**Fennel Sausage (makes 1½ cups/375 mL,
enough for 3 pizzas)**
½ pound (225 g) ground pork
2 cloves garlic, minced
1½ teaspoons (7 mL) fennel seeds, toasted
1 teaspoon (5 mL) red chili flakes
½ teaspoon (2 mL) kosher salt
½ teaspoon (2 mL) freshly ground pepper

Pizza
1 ball pizza dough, shaped as directed on
    page 139
½ cup (125 mL) Red Sauce (page 259)
1 cup (250 mL) shredded mozzarella
    cheese
½ cup (125 mL) thinly sliced red onion
¼ cup (60 mL) seeded and thinly sliced
    long red chili
½ sweet red pepper, roasted, peeled, and
    thickly sliced
1 teaspoon (5 mL) dried basil, for garnish

1. To make the Fennel Sausage, preheat the oven to 350°F (180°C). Have ready a small casserole dish or baking dish at least 3 inches (8 cm) high.

2. In a large bowl, combine the ground pork, garlic, fennel seeds, chili flakes, salt, and pepper; mix well. Press into the casserole dish. Bake, uncovered, for 20 minutes, or until the internal temperature reaches 160°F (70°C). Allow to cool slightly so you don't burn your fingers. Crumble into 1-inch (2.5 cm) chunks and set aside. Leftover sausage can be tightly covered and refrigerated for up to 4 days or in a resealable plastic bag and freeze for up to 1 month.

3. Place a pizza stone on the top shelf of the oven and increase the oven to 550°F (290°C) or the highest setting. Let the stone heat for an additional 30 minutes after the oven has reached its set temperature. (If you don't have a pizza stone, you can use a rimless baking sheet.)

4. Generously flour a pizza peel or rimless baking sheet. Transfer the stretched dough to the peel or tray and give it a shake to ensure the dough is not sticking to it. Evenly spread the Red Sauce over the pizza dough, stopping about 1 inch (2.5 cm) from the edge. Scatter the mozzarella evenly over the sauce, then top with ½ cup (125 mL) of the Fennel Sausage, the onions, chilies, and roasted red pepper.

5. To transfer the pizza to the stone, place the peel over the stone and quickly pull the peel back towards you. (Or lift out the hot baking sheet, slide the pizza onto it, and return to the oven.) Bake for 9 minutes (or 11 minutes if baking on a baking sheet), or until the edges are slightly charred and crispy. Keep a close eye on it.

6. Use the pizza peel to remove the pizza to a cutting board. Garnish with dried basil. Slice and serve immediately.

MAINS

ALICE WATERS

CHEZ PANISSE, BERKELEY, CALIFORNIA

Alice Waters, chef and restaurateur, is the root of our culinary family tree. She is the founder of Chez Panisse, a restaurant that opened in 1971 and has become a mecca for foodies, chefs, and locavores. Chez Panisse is a place where people come together with friends and family to eat delicious, thoughtfully prepared food. In our minds, Alice and her staff have created the perfect restaurant, something we aspire to every day.

"If you want to be the best, you have to train with the best." Truer words have never been spoken, so fresh out of cooking school, Jeff packed his bags and headed out West. His internship at Chez Panisse set Jeff on a career path that has lasted twenty years. And it was his experience there, under the watchful eyes of chefs David Tanis and Russell Moore, that affect what we do at Bread Bar—offering our guests thoughtful food with respect for where it came from, simply and honestly.

You can say that we are still students of the culinary arts. We are fans of haute cuisine chefs like Alain Passard (L'Arpège) and Thomas Keller (The French Laundry), as well as molecular gastronomy cooks such as Heston Blumenthal (The Fat Duck) and Grant Achatz (Alinea) and food writers such as Elizabeth David and Richard Olney. But it was the food that Jeff cooked at Chez Panisse that has lingered on his palate and fuels his passion to be a chef. The freshness, the intense and unadorned flavours, and Alice Waters's focus on seasonal ingredients—the eventual hallmarks of California cuisine—were the foundations of Jeff's cooking

philosophy. With a collection of over a thousand cookbooks strewn across each restaurant, home, and office, the very first cookbook Jeff bought was Waters's *Chez Panisse Cooking*. That stained and dog-eared book, with its duct-taped spine, now lives on a shelf at Bread Bar, and we are still consulting it for inspiration.

Jeff's love affair with the food at Chez Panisse energized his desire to learn about food as opposed to just eating it. Adding the appreciation of local farmers and food artisans was nothing less than a revelation. But it wasn't until he attended a Slow Food event in Bra, Italy, that he truly understood how to value food.

The seminar was a tasting and talk with the top prosciutto producers in Italy. When a plate of ten different sliced prosciuttos arrived, Jeff proceeded to eat them all, appreciatively. Then he sat solemn, watching as the class picked up each slice one at a time, held it up to the light, smelled it, and rubbed it between their fingers.

The class evaluated, discussed, and fully appreciated the artful work in ham production—all this before actually tasting it. This mindful savouring of a single ingredient was a moment of learning for Jeff. And this appreciation has become somewhat of an obsession for him since then. Jeff is constantly looking for the beauty in our food. Getting pleasure from our food is a bit of a lost art in our modern world. There is no scarcity or any real appreciation of what is in season or what is a local tradition. What happens now is that Jeff shows up at Bread Bar one day with shockingly fresh king salmon (yes, salmon has a season), and another day, with hand foraged wild leeks (ramps) in one hand and a bag of fiddleheads in the other.

While Alice was creating what Chez Panisse would become, she first started with the need to eat the food she had enjoyed while studying abroad in France. At that time, finding ripe goat cheese, freshly baked baguettes, or tender green peas was not as easy as it is today. Health food stores existed in Berkeley, but tofu and ancient grains were not scratching that itch. This led her to seek out the flavours stuck in her mind by creating a network of backyard gardeners, food artisans, and like-minded cooks. In the early years Chez Panisse's menu was written as a typical French bistro, with French dishes using French-inspired ingredients, written in French. Naturally her net-work of suppliers could only deliver to the kitchen what would grow in Northern California. Over time the chefs creating the menus (Jeremiah Tower) began to look locally for inspiration. Dover sole was replaced with local sand dabs as the fish course, and Mission figs found their way into the salad course. California cuisine, as we now know it, was taking shape. Then in the fall of 1976, Chez Panisse offered its first local, regional dinner, based on regions of France like Provence, Burgundy, or Brittany, but on Northern California! This was a tipping point in terms of how we all eat today. This menu featured Tomales Bay oysters, Mendocino-style corn soup, Monterey Bay prawns, Big Sur trout, and fresh figs from the local farmers' market.

Over the years, chefs and consumers took notice. Backyard harvesters, farmers' markets, and food artisans throughout North America have Alice and community to thank for what she calls this delicious revolution.

This is also something we work on at Bread Bar. We, too, have created a network of local suppliers, farmers, and like-minded staff. A myriad of suppliers means lots of time on the phone and emailing, and it can get quite complicated. But, as I am sure Alice Waters would agree, it is much more satisfying at the end of the day.

A favourite anecdote about Alice Waters is how she often chooses a choice piece of fruit as a dessert—a gorgeous, blushing peach whose juice drips down your chin, or a bowl of jewel-like raspberries that make your jaw ache with their intense flavour. She lets the ingredients speak for themselves. These days, Chez Panisse can get away with offering a simple, perfect peach as a dessert option. Perhaps this fruitful revelation is the next step in the evolution of Bread Bar—at least, this is what we are working towards.

After fifteen or so years of working together, we've mastered a certain creative tension that gives us room to disagree. Jeff is good at making on-the-spot decisions; Bettina needs time to mull things over. But our unwritten agreement is that we think thoughtful food is our priority. We may not agree on much, but one thing we do agree on completely is that Alice Waters and her philosophy are our greatest inspirations.

RIPENED
ON THE VINE

In recent years we have witnessed a terrific shift in how people buy food. Though they still shop for basics in mainstream grocery stores, the move towards buying local produce from farmers' markets has intensified, especially as those markets have grown and flourished in urban settings. People want food that hasn't been tampered with chemically or physically, and buying local produce feeds into that demand.

When it comes to food choices, Jeff's main reason for shopping at a farmers' market is, as he puts it, "the food has been ripened on the vine, not ripened on the truck." Though hard to believe, many varieties of fruits and vegetables are selected for their ability to ripen on a truck as well as to survive travel with as few bruises as possible. In some cases, produce even goes through a gassing process to stimulate the ripening process.

When you shop at a farmers' market you can feel confident that farmers and other producers are going to be selling you the most delicious, sun-drenched product possible. Most of the mouth-watering options are picked and sold at their peak. But the benefits of shopping this way don't stop there. In this producer-to-consumer setting, you can easily develop a lasting relationship with the farmers. You can ask them about how their produce is grown, whether pesticides or herbicides were used, or if the produce is farmed organically. As restaurateurs, we can use this knowledge to make informed choices about purchasing products to highlight on our menu. We learn what is perfectly ripe at that moment, as well as finding out what will be harvested next. This kind of advance knowledge is key to menu planning, whether you're a restaurant chef planning for a season or a home cook who has a week of meals to put together.

Another positive result of shopping at farmers' markets is the deep engagement that develops between the local economy and the community. We never expected this benefit to become part of what we do as a restaurant business. Initially we were only looking for the best possible food products. Once we learned how much we were increasing supply and demand and creating a positive environment for local commerce, it became a way of life. Every summer we purchase produce from Backyard Harvest, run by a local farmer, who grows produce in neighbourhood backyards, many of them within twelve blocks of Bread Bar in Hamilton. The produce is often picked only hours before we receive it. FoxHole Farm supplies tomatoes specifically for our tomato salad. But they're so delicious we'll take all the tomatoes the farm has to offer and put them in every dish we can— other salads, pizzas, and daily specials.

One amazing perk of running a restaurant is the joy of accepting food when it shows up at the back door. Local farmers who are peddling their wares drop by unannounced, and suddenly we have a new ingredient to serve. Limited-season produce like garlic scapes or foraged mushrooms show up, and we can't say yes fast enough. All of it can be used, even if it can't be transformed into a dish that day. We can process a bumper crop of arugula as pesto. An overabundance of strawberries can be turned into coulis for use in milkshakes all year round. This adaptability and versatility makes it possible for Bread Bar to deliver seasonal ingredients—picked and processed at the peak of freshness—all year round.

Farmers' markets usually don't run all year, so shop while you can. The fruits and vegetables always taste better, and who knows what other delicious things you might find. The markets often host artisan craftspeople selling everything from local honeys and jams to fresh breads and pies, cheeses, eggs, and organically produced meats. Exploring a local market will lead you to many discoveries, many that will knock your socks off! Above all else, farmers' markets are simply a special place to spend time with family and friends and connect with people in your community.

1. To prepare the chicken, place it on a cutting board, breast side down and with the legs closest to you. Using a sturdy knife or kitchen scissors, cut along each side of the backbone to remove it entirely. Turn the chicken skin side up and, using your hands, press down hard on the breastbone to make the chicken as flat as possible.

2. In a small bowl, stir together the garlic, rosemary, 1 tablespoon (15 mL) of the olive oil, and salt and pepper to taste. Rub this all over the skin of the chicken. Transfer the chicken to a platter, cover, and refrigerate overnight.

3. Preheat the oven to 400°F (200°C).

4. Heat the remaining 2 tablespoons (30 mL) olive oil in a large, heavy skillet over medium heat. Place the chicken in the skillet, skin side down, along with any of the rosemary-garlic rub that may have fallen off. Place another heavy skillet on top of the chicken. The idea is to flatten the chicken so you get evenly cooked meat with a maximum amount of crisp skin.

5. Cook for 8 minutes. Remove the top skillet and transfer the chicken to the oven. Roast for 15 minutes more. Turn the chicken skin side up and roast for 10 minutes more, or until the internal temperature of the thigh reads 160°F (70°C). Let rest for at least 15 minutes before serving.

6. While the chicken is resting, make the Watermelon and Pecan Salad. Cut the flesh of the watermelon into 1-inch (2.5 cm) cubes (you should have about 5 cups/1.25 L). In a medium bowl, combine the watermelon, pecans, House Vinaigrette, mint, and chili flakes. Season with salt and pepper. Tip out onto a platter and evenly distribute the feta over the salad.

7. Carve the chicken and garnish with lime wedges. Serve the chicken and salad side by side so your guests can help themselves.

ROAST CHICKEN WITH WATERMELON AND PECAN SALAD

SERVES 4 · REQUIRES TIME FOR PREP

This roast chicken is welcome at the table any time of year. Here we pair it with a watermelon salad that perfectly captures summer. In fall and winter, we serve it with garlic mashed potatoes or Spicy Lentil, Wild Rice, and Orzo Salad (page 71).

Roast Chicken
1 organic chicken (3½ pounds/1.6 kg)
2 cloves garlic, chopped
1 tablespoon (15 mL) minced fresh rosemary
3 tablespoons (45 mL) extra-virgin olive oil, divided
Kosher salt and freshly ground pepper
1 lime, cut into wedges, for garnish

Watermelon and Pecan Salad
1 small seedless watermelon
¾ cup (175 mL) toasted pecans, crushed
¼ cup (60 mL) House Vinaigrette (page 244)
1 tablespoon (15 mL) minced fresh mint
½ teaspoon (2 mL) red chili flakes
Kosher salt and freshly ground pepper
1 cup (250 mL) crumbled feta cheese

BRAISED CHICKEN THIGHS WITH GREEN OLIVES AND PAPPARDELLE

SERVES 4 • REQUIRES TIME FOR PREP

We love to cook this wonderful dish at home. As the chicken braises, all the beautiful flavours get mixed together. It is so versatile that it goes well with pasta, rice, or seasonal vegetables. If you prefer a little heat on your plate, add a heaping tablespoon of Jalapeño Pesto (page 258) when you add the pasta.

---

8 chicken thighs, trimmed of excess skin and fat
2 bay leaves
1 clove garlic, minced
2 tablespoons (30 mL) chopped fresh thyme
1½ teaspoons (7 mL) red chili flakes
Kosher salt and freshly ground pepper
3 tablespoons (45 mL) canola oil
¾ cup (175 mL) dry white wine
1 cup (250 mL) diced white onion
12 Castelvetrano olives or other mild, crunchy green olives
¾ teaspoon (4 mL) Dijon mustard
1 cup (250 mL) chicken stock
1 pound (450 g) dried pappardelle
1 tablespoon (15 mL) chopped fresh flat-leaf parsley
5 slices lemon

1. Place the chicken in a large freezer bag and add the bay leaves, garlic, thyme, and chili flakes. Seal the bag, give the chicken a massage to distribute the herbs, and refrigerate overnight.

2. Preheat the oven to 375°F (190°C).

3. Remove the chicken from the bag, pat it dry with paper towels, and season well on both sides with salt and pepper. Heat the canola oil in a medium Dutch oven over high heat. Reduce the heat to medium and add the chicken, skin side down. Sear until the skin is a deep golden brown, 8 to 10 minutes. Remove the chicken and set aside.

4. Add the white wine and onion to the pot. Cook, stirring occasionally, until the onions are translucent and tender, about 10 minutes. Remove from the heat and stir in the olives and mustard.

5. Place the chicken skin side up on top of the onion mixture. Add the chicken stock. Push the chicken down so it is nestled in among the onions and stock. Place in the oven, uncovered, and braise for about 40 minutes, turning the chicken twice. To test for doneness, pierce the meat near the bone with a small knife; the juices should run clear. Remove the chicken and set aside.

6. Bring a large pot of salted water to a rolling boil over high heat. Drop the pasta into the water and cook for 8 minutes, stirring often. It is done when a noodle is soft with a remaining bit of firmness when bitten.

7. Using tongs, lift out the cooked pasta and add it to the hot onions; stir until the pasta is coated in onions. If the sauce looks a bit dry, splash in a little pasta water. Season with salt and pepper.

8. Nestle the chicken in the pasta. Garnish the dish with parsley and lemon slices and serve immediately.

1. Place the chicken in a large freezer bag and add the Master Brine. Seal the bag, pressing out as much air as possible to ensure all the meat is in contact with the brine. Refrigerate overnight.

2. Set up a steamer on the stovetop. Drain the chicken and discard the brine. Put the chicken in the steamer basket. Turn the heat to medium and cover. Steam the chicken for 40 minutes, or until the internal temperature of a thigh reaches 160°F (70°C). Remove from the steamer and set aside to cool. (The steamed chicken can be refrigerated, covered, for up to 3 days before frying.)

3. In a large bowl, combine the flour, potato starch, salt, garlic powder, onion powder, paprika, and cayenne. Pour the buttermilk into a separate large bowl.

4. Add the chicken to the buttermilk, turning to completely coat. Then, working one piece at a time, dredge the chicken in the flour mixture, pressing and turning so the flour sticks to all sides. If you like a thick crust, repeat the process with each piece of chicken, starting in the buttermilk. Place the chicken on a platter and chill for 1 hour.

5. Fit a large, heavy pot with a deep-fat thermometer and pour in enough canola oil to come halfway up the sides. Heat the oil over medium-high to 350°F (180°C). Carefully add the chicken and fry, turning often and adjusting the heat to maintain the temperature, until deep golden brown and the internal temperature is 160°F (70°C), about 8 minutes. Transfer the chicken to paper towels to drain. Season with salt, drizzle with the honey, and serve immediately.

BUTTERMILK FRIED CHICKEN

SERVES 4 · REQUIRES TIME FOR PREP

This recipe modifies for the home kitchen a two-part technique we use at the restaurant to make an unforgettable fried chicken. Brining the chicken first helps retain moisture and seasons the meat throughout. Then, gently steaming the chicken (to mimic the sous vide cooking we do at the restaurant) precooks it perfectly, so you only have to fry it for about 8 minutes, as opposed to 20 minutes or so with the traditional deep-frying method. We often pair this dish with the Watermelon and Pecan Salad (page 167).

1 organic chicken (3 pounds/1.35 kg), cut into 8 pieces (2 thighs, 2 drumsticks, breasts cut in half with wings attached)
1 batch Master Brine (page 250)
1½ cups (375 mL) all-purpose flour
½ cup (125 mL) potato starch or cornstarch
2 tablespoons (30 mL) kosher salt
1 tablespoon (15 mL) garlic powder
1 tablespoon (15 mL) onion powder
1 tablespoon (15 mL) sweet paprika
1 teaspoon (5 mL) cayenne pepper
2 cups (500 mL) buttermilk
Canola oil, for deep-frying
1 tablespoon (15 mL) liquid honey

BAVETTE STEAK COOKED ON CHARCOAL

SERVES 4

If you want to take grilling to a new level, ditch the grate and cook directly on the coals. The result is a serious char on the outside and a moist, deliciously smoky interior. Bavette steak—also known as flap steak in North America—is a very beefy cut taken from the bottom sirloin, with good beef flavour and moderate tenderness at a pretty good price. This steak is perfectly paired with a Kale Caesar Salad (page 62).

For grilling, you'll need 5 to 6 pounds (2.25 to 2.7 kg) of hardwood lump charcoal. We use lighter fluid to start the fire. Despite its bad reputation, lighter fluid is an acceptable choice. If you wait until the coals are covered with white-grey ash before you start cooking, all the fluid will be burned off long before you put anything on or over the fire, so it has no effect on the food.

Steak Rub

½ cup (125 mL) beer (we use Beau's
   Lug-Tread lagered ale)
2 cloves garlic, minced
1 teaspoon (5 mL) chili powder
1 teaspoon (5 mL) freshly ground pepper
½ teaspoon (2 mL) ground cumin
½ teaspoon (2 mL) kosher salt

Steak

1 bavette steak (2 pounds/900 g and 1 to
   1½ inches/2.5 to 4 cm thick)
4 large carrots
4 green onions
Kosher salt and freshly ground pepper
Olive oil

1. To make the Steak Rub, in a small bowl, combine the beer, garlic, chili powder, pepper, cumin, and salt. Mix to make a paste and set aside.

2. Arrange lump charcoal in a pile. Sprinkle with lighter fluid. Wait 1 minute for the fluid to soak in. Light the pile in several places. Wait until the charcoal is covered in white ash before cooking, about 20 minutes.

3. When the coals are ready, pat the steak all over with the rub. This will protect the steak from the coals. Spread out the coals evenly, and give the bed a good blow to remove most of the ash. Carefully place the steak and the carrots on the coals.

4. Cook the steak and carrots, turning every 5 minutes, for about 15 minutes. The steak and carrots will develop a black char—don't fear this. The steak will be done medium when the internal temperature is 125°F (50°C). (Bavette is best cooked medium-rare or medium, not rare, which is quite chewy.) The carrots are done when they can be easily pierced with a knife. Remove the steak and carrots from the charcoal and set aside. Let the steak rest for at least 10 minutes so the juices have a chance to redistribute throughout the meat.

5. Meanwhile, place the green onions on the coals and cook, turning frequently, about 5 minutes. Remove from the coals.

6. With the back of a knife, scrape the char off the carrots to reveal the bright orange flesh. Season with salt, pepper, and a drizzle of olive oil.

7. Brush the ash off the steak with a pastry brush or kitchen cloth. Slice the steak against the grain and season each piece with salt, pepper, and a drizzle of olive oil. Season the green onions with salt, pepper, and a drizzle of olive oil as well. Serve.

Vegetables you can cook on coals

Cabbage Rub a head of cabbage with olive oil and roast it directly in the coals, turning often until the outside is charred and the cabbage is easily pierced with a knife, about 1 hour.

Potatoes Rub large potatoes with olive oil and roast them directly in the coals. Wrap smaller potatoes, such as fingerlings, in foil along with butter, olive oil, garlic, and fresh herbs. Roast potatoes for about 40 minutes, or until easily pierced with a fork.

Asparagus Wrap asparagus in foil with olive oil and fresh herbs and roast until tender, 8 to 12 minutes, depending on the thickness of the spears.

Fennel Wrap a trimmed fennel bulb in foil and roast it until blackened and tender, 35 to 45 minutes.

Beets Wrap beets in foil or brush them with olive oil and roast them directly in the coals until tender. Either way, it takes about 1½ hours to roast baseball-size beets.

Eggplant Rub eggplant with olive oil and roast directly in the coals until the outside is thoroughly burnt, turning frequently, about 30 minutes. Char-grilled eggplant makes an amazingly smokey baba ganoush.

PIRI PIRI BABY BACK RIBS

Summertime to us means outdoor cooking, barbecues, and good times. If we had to cook just one thing in the summer, it would be these simple, flavourful, and tender ribs. They are easy to cook and are the perfect outdoor dinner with friends. Apple cider brings both sweetness and the moisture needed for the long, slow cooking. Serve these with Heirloom Tomato Salad (page 58), Peach and Mozzarella Salad (page 68), or Coleslaw (page 72).

---

4 racks baby back ribs (about 8 pounds/ 3.5 kg)
1 cup (250 mL) Piri Piri Dry Rub (page 265)
1 cup (250 mL) dry apple cider

1. Place the ribs meat side down on a cutting board and remove the membrane from the back of the rack by inserting a small knife beneath it and pulling it up so you can grab it with a dish towel. Peel off the membrane and discard.

2. In a large bowl, combine the ribs and the Piri Piri Dry Rub. Using your hands, cover the meat entirely in the rub. Shake off excess. Wrap ribs in plastic wrap and refrigerate for at least 3 hours or overnight.

3. Preheat the oven to 325°F (160°C).

4. Place the ribs in a large Dutch oven—it's okay if they overlap—and add the apple cider. Cover tightly and bake for 4 hours, or until the meat is fork-tender. Uncover and let cool. (At this point you can wrap the ribs in plastic wrap and refrigerate for up to 1 week or freeze in a resealable plastic bag for up to 1 month.)

5. To serve, preheat a grill to medium-high. Grill the ribs for 5 minutes per side, until slightly charred. You can serve these ribs dry, by sprinkling with a little more Piri Piri Dry Rub, or wet with your favourite barbecue sauce.

ROASTED LAMB SHOULDER WITH POLENTA AND GREEN OLIVE TAPENADE

SERVES 6 • REQUIRES TIME FOR PREP

This recipe is going to show you how utterly incredible a slow-roasted shoulder of lamb can be. Once you try a tender, juicy lamb shoulder, you will question why you spend so much money on the ever-popular rack of lamb. Shoulder is a favourite cut of ours because it is the most flavourful and, if cooked correctly, the most tender. Serve this with Green Beans with Miso Dressing (page 75) in summer or Apple and Walnut Salad (page 50) in fall.

1. In a large bowl, stir together the olive oil, rosemary, garlic, and salt. Add the lamb and rub it all over with the marinade. Cover and refrigerate overnight.

2. Preheat the oven to 325°F (160°C).

3. Place the lamb in a high-sided roasting pan that fits it fairly snugly. If the pan is too large, the braising liquid could burn. Cover with foil and roast for 4 hours. Increase the heat to 400°F (200°C), remove the foil, and continue to roast until the lamb has a nice char, about 20 minutes. When the meat is done, you can pull it apart easily with two forks.

4. While the lamb is charring, make the Soft Polenta. In a large saucepan, bring the stock to a simmer. Whisk in the cornmeal in a slow, thin stream. (This will prevent the polenta from clumping.) Simmer, stirring occasionally, until the polenta is thickened and starts to pull away from the sides of the pan, about 30 minutes. Remove from the heat and stir in the butter and Parmesan.

5. Serve the lamb and the polenta with the Green Olive Tapenade on the side.

3 tablespoons (45 mL) olive oil
Leaves from 5 sprigs fresh rosemary, chopped
4 cloves garlic, minced
1 tablespoon (15 mL) kosher salt
1 bone-in lamb shoulder (4½ pounds/2 kg)

Soft Polenta
6 cups (1.5 L) chicken or beef stock
1½ cups (375 mL) coarse cornmeal
4 tablespoons (60 mL) unsalted butter
¼ cup (60 mL) grated Parmesan cheese

For Serving
1 cup (250 mL) Green Olive Tapenade (page 255)

GRILLED LAMB CHOPS WITH SAFFRON RISOTTO

SERVES 4

This risotto is a simple and humble dish, except for the one ingredient that happens to be the most expensive on the planet by weight—saffron. Thankfully, you don't need much to achieve a brilliant yellow colour and distinctive flavour. We love lamb loin chops for their nice meaty flavour; they're basically the T-bone steak of lamb. Pair this dish with our White Gazpacho (page 40) for a light spring dinner.

8 lamb loin chops (1¼ inches/3 cm thick)

Saffron Risotto
6 cups (1.5 L) chicken stock
2 tablespoons (30 mL) olive oil
1 white onion, minced
1 cup (250 mL) arborio rice
½ cup (125 mL) dry white wine
½ teaspoon (2 mL) saffron threads
1 cup (250 mL) grated Parmesan cheese
¼ cup (60 mL) heavy (35%) cream
2 tablespoons (30 mL) unsalted butter
Kosher salt and freshly ground pepper

1. To make the Saffron Risotto, in a saucepan, bring the chicken stock to a simmer; keep hot. Heat the olive oil in a medium saucepan over medium heat. Reduce the heat to medium, add the onion and cook, stirring occasionally, until the onions are translucent and tender, about 10 minutes. Add the rice and cook, stirring, until the grains look slightly translucent, about 2 minutes.

2. Add the white wine and saffron threads and cook, stirring, until the wine has all been absorbed, about 6 minutes.

3. Add 1 cup (250 mL) of the hot chicken stock and cook, stirring constantly, until the rice has absorbed most of the stock. Continue to add the stock, 1 cup (250 mL) at a time, whenever the rice mixture looks stiff, stirring continuously until the rice is creamy and tender, about 30 minutes total. Remove from the heat and stir in the Parmesan, cream, and butter. Season with salt and pepper. Cover and let stand.

4. Preheat a grill to high.

5. Season the lamb chops generously with salt and pepper. Grill, turning often, for 8 minutes, or until the internal temperature reaches 130°F (55°C) for medium doneness. Remove from the grill and set aside to rest for at least 8 minutes. Gently reheat the Saffron Risotto and serve together.

OVERNIGHT BBQ BRISKET

SERVES 10 • REQUIRES TIME FOR PREP

We have an enviable offset smoker, the kind that's big enough it sits on a trailer. We can smoke ten whole briskets at once, it is that cool and fun. This is a modified version of our BBQ brisket that can deliver to your friends and family a party-sized helping of butter-like tender beef with very little effort. The onions bring both sweetness and the moisture needed for the long, slow cooking. Note that you need three days to prepare this brisket. (Trust us, it's worth it.) We serve this with Coleslaw (page 72) and White Pan Bread (page 18).

1. Place the brisket in a large roasting pan. In a small bowl, stir together the salt, pepper, brown sugar, cumin seeds, and paprika. Spread this mixture evenly all over the brisket, pressing down with your palm so it adheres. Gently shake off any excess. Cover and refrigerate overnight.

2. The next day, preheat the oven to 250°F (120°C).

3. Remove the brisket from the roasting pan, scatter the onions, garlic, and carrots in the pan, and place the brisket on top of the vegetables. Drizzle the barbecue sauce all over the top of the brisket (as if you were icing a cake). Pour the water down the side of the pan (not over the brisket). Cover tightly with foil and place in the oven to cook, unattended, for 8 hours, until tender.

4. At this point the brisket will be almost half its original size, so if you prefer, you can transfer it to a smaller vessel. Strain the cooking liquid over the brisket and discard the vegetables. Let cool, then cover and refrigerate overnight.

5. The next day, transfer the brisket to a cutting board, with the wide side facing you. Brisket has grain that runs in 2 different directions: the thin end (the flat) slices north to south, while the fatty end (the point) slices east to west. With a sharp knife, slice the meat against the grain. At this point you can reheat the meat, wrapped in foil on a medium-low grill or in a 400°F (200°C) oven. Serve with more barbecue sauce and all your favourite accompaniments.

1 brisket, both flat and point (7 pounds/ 3.15 kg), trimmed of fat
½ cup (125 mL) kosher salt
½ cup (125 mL) freshly ground pepper
2 tablespoons (30 mL) lightly packed brown sugar
1 tablespoon (15 mL) cumin seeds, toasted
1 tablespoon (15 mL) smoked paprika
3 medium onions, thickly sliced
5 cloves garlic, smashed
2 carrots, peeled and chopped
2 cups (500 mL) your favourite barbecue sauce (we use JC's BBQ Sauce, page 262)
2 cups (500 mL) water

PORK CHOPS WITH SAGE AND BALSAMIC VINEGAR

Everyone needs to be able to cook a pork chop. It is truly one of the finer things in life, especially now that heritage breeds of pigs are becoming more common. This is not only good news for biodiversity on farms but also for you, the consumer, as heritage breeds tend to have much more fat on them, which makes for a better-tasting chop. Berkshire, Tamworth, and Red Wattle are three to look for. Besides that, we think the combination of pork, sage, and balsamic vinegar is perfect. Serve these chops with steamed French green beans and Saffron Risotto (page 180).

4 bone-in rib or loin pork chops (10 ounces/ 280 g each), untrimmed
2 cups (500 mL) Master Brine (page 250)
6 tablespoons (90 mL) canola oil
1 tablespoon (15 mL) all-purpose flour
12 fresh sage leaves
Juice of 1 lemon
1 tablespoon (15 mL) unsalted butter
1 tablespoon (15 mL) balsamic vinegar
Kosher salt and freshly ground pepper

1. Place the pork chops in a large freezer bag and add the Master Brine. Seal the bag, pressing out as much air as possible to ensure all the meat is in contact with the brine. Refrigerate for 12 hours.

2. Heat the canola oil in a large, heavy skillet over medium-high heat. Remove the chops from the brine and discard the brine. Dry the chops well with paper towel. Dust the chops lightly with flour (to develop a nice crust).

3. Add enough chops to the pan so they are close together but not touching. Turn the heat down a little. Cook the pork chops without moving them, save for turning them once, for about 7 minutes on each side. You are looking for a deep brown crust on each side. Set the chops aside on a plate. Repeat with the remaining chops.

4. Remove the skillet from the heat and add the sage, lemon juice, butter, and balsamic vinegar. Stir a bit so the flavours blend, but don't let the butter melt completely. Season with salt and pepper.

5. Divide the chops among plates, spoon the sauce over the chops, and serve.

GARGANELLI WITH RED PEPPERS AND PINE NUTS

SERVES 6

This recipe uses the restaurant standby of stirring hot, almost cooked pasta into a sauce in a separate
pan, which finishes cooking the pasta and adds a depth of flavour that is hard to describe.
If you want to spice things up, add 2 tablespoons (30 mL) of Chili Confit (page 253).
Adding Fennel Sausage (page 158) turns this dish into a hearty dinner.

3 sweet red peppers
¼ cup (60 mL) olive oil
4 anchovy fillets in oil, minced
3 cloves garlic, chopped
½ cup (125 mL) dry white wine
4 leaves kale, stemmed and coarsely
    chopped
1 teaspoon (5 mL) red chili flakes
1 pound (450 g) garganelli
Kosher salt and freshly ground pepper
2 tablespoons (30 mL) pine nuts
1 tablespoon (15 mL) minced fresh flat-leaf
    parsley
3 ounces (85 g) Parmigiano-Reggiano
    cheese

1. Preheat a grill or broiler to high. Grill the red peppers,
   turning often with tongs, until blistered and blackened
   on all sides, about 15 minutes. Alternatively, roast the
   peppers directly over the stovetop flame of a gas oven.
   Transfer to a large bowl, cover with plastic wrap, and let
   steam for 20 minutes. Peel the peppers and chop them
   into ½-inch (1 cm) pieces.

2. Heat the olive oil in a large skillet over medium-high
   heat. Add the anchovies and garlic and cook for 1 minute.
   Stir in the chopped red peppers, then add the white
   wine. Boil until the pan is nearly dry. Stir in the kale and
   chili flakes. Remove from the heat.

3. Bring a large pot of water to a boil, add salt, and drop in
   the pasta. Cook for about 9 minutes or until the pasta is
   tender. You will be cooking it further in the sauce. Drain,
   reserving some of the pasta water. Return the sauce to
   medium-high heat and stir in the pasta. Cook for 5 minutes,
   to allow the flavours to mingle. Add a spoonful of pasta
   water if the sauce looks too dry. Remove from the heat.

4. Season with salt and pepper. Add the pine nuts and
   parsley and toss well. Tip into a large serving bowl,
   garnish with an over-generous grating of Parmigiano-
   Reggiano, and serve immediately.

MAC AND CHEESE

SERVES 6

Mac and cheese ranks right up there as the ultimate in comfort food. Like many popular dishes, though, this one has suffered from its success—or more to the point, *we* have suffered, by consuming poorly made versions. Back to the basics, everyone! Make this with your kids and they will never want KD again. We serve this with any of our salads on the side. Try the Kale Caesar Salad (page 62) or the Roasted Asparagus with Manchego Cheese (page 73).

1. Preheat the oven to 375°F (190°C). Generously grease a 13- x 9-inch (3.5 L) baking dish with 1 tablespoon (15 mL) of the butter.

2. Bring a large pot of water to a boil, add salt, and drop in the pasta. Cook for about 9 minutes or until the pasta is tender. Drain.

3. In a large bowl, toss together the cheddar and Monterey Jack cheese. Set aside 2 cups (500 mL) for the topping.

4. To the cheese mixture, add the pasta, White Sauce, bacon, Caramelized Onions, and salt and pepper to taste. Mix well. Turn this mixture into the greased baking dish, pressing the pasta down to form a smooth, even top.

5. In a small bowl, combine the panko crumbs and reserved cheese. Evenly cover the pasta with the panko crumbs and cheese mixture. Dot with the remaining 2 tablespoons (30 mL) butter. Bake, uncovered, for 25 minutes, or until bubbling and crusty on top.

3 tablespoons (45 mL) unsalted butter, divided
1 pound (450 g) macaroni
12 ounces (340 g) sharp cheddar cheese, grated, divided
12 ounces (340 g) Monterey Jack cheese, grated, divided
1 cup (250 mL) White Sauce (page 259)
4 strips bacon, cooked crisp and chopped (about 1 cup/250 mL)
3 tablespoons (45 mL) Caramelized Onions (page 250)
Kosher salt and freshly ground pepper
⅔ cup (150 mL) panko crumbs

SPAGHETTI ARRABBIATA

SERVES 4

This is an easy pasta dish, and a delicious one to whip up on a weeknight—it will make you feel like you are sitting in the hills of Sicily. We kick it up a notch with some chili confit. Serve this pasta with the Arugula and Fennel Salad (page 49) or a toasted slice of Rosemary Focaccia (page 22), or before the Roasted Lamb Shoulder with Polenta and Green Olive Tapenade (page 179).

1½ cups (375 mL) ricotta cheese, drained well

2 tablespoons (30 mL) heavy (35%) cream

1 teaspoon (5 mL) grated lemon zest

2 cups (500 mL) Red Sauce (page 259)

6 fresh basil leaves

3 tablespoons (45 mL) unsalted butter

12 ounces (340 g) spaghetti

Kosher salt and freshly ground pepper

3 tablespoons (45 mL) Chili Confit (page 253)

2 tablespoons (30 mL) extra-virgin olive oil

Chopped fresh flat-leaf parsley

1. Bring a large pot of salted water to a boil over high heat.

2. In a medium bowl, whisk together the ricotta, cream, and lemon zest until light and airy. Set aside.

3. In a medium skillet over medium heat, bring the Red Sauce to a simmer. Stir in the basil leaves and butter. Remove from the heat and keep warm.

4. Drop the pasta into the boiling water and cook at a rolling boil for about 5 minutes, stirring often. It is done when a noodle is soft with a remaining bit of firmness when bitten.

5. Using tongs, lift out the cooked pasta and add it to the Red Sauce; stir well. Return the sauce to medium heat and cook for about 5 minutes, to allow the spaghetti to absorb some of the sauce. Splash in a little pasta water if the sauce looks too dry. Season with salt and pepper.

6. Divide the pasta among 4 plates. Top with equal portions of the ricotta mixture, Chili Confit, olive oil, and parsley. Serve immediately.

DELICATA SQUASH WITH SPROUTED CHICKPEAS

SERVES 6

Mastering the art of roasting a squash will serve you well in the cold nights of winter when the cupboard is bare. Hearty and meaty, this dish is a vegetarian's Sunday roast. To speed things along, use canned chickpeas. White or black beans are also delicious treated this way.

6 small Delicata squash (about 1 pound/
450 g each)
Kosher salt and freshly ground pepper
4 tablespoons (60 mL) unsalted butter
2 onions, diced
1 bunch kale (about 1 pound/450 g),
stemmed and chopped
1 cup (250 mL) sprouted chickpeas
1 cup (250 mL) cooked green lentils
1 teaspoon (5 mL) Za'atar Spice Blend
(page 265) or store-bought
½ teaspoon (2 mL) ground coriander
Chopped fresh flat-leaf parsley, for garnish

1. Preheat the oven to 425°F (220°C).

2. Cut each squash in half lengthwise and spoon out and discard the seeds. Sprinkle the cut side of the squash with salt and pepper, then place them on a greased baking sheet cut side down. Roast for 25 minutes, or until the squash is easily pierced with a knife. Let cool slightly.

3. While the squash is cooking, melt the butter in a medium saucepan over medium-high heat until foaming. Reduce the heat to medium, add the onions, and cook, stirring occasionally, until the onions are translucent and tender, about 10 minutes. Add the kale, chickpeas, lentils, Za'atar Spice Blend, and coriander; mix well. Cook, stirring frequently, for about 8 minutes, or until the chickpeas and lentils are tender. Remove from the heat.

4. Reduce the oven to 350°F (180°C). Turn the squash cut side up and divide the stuffing between the squash. Bake until everything is piping hot, about 10 minutes. Garnish with fresh parsley and serve.

LING COD WITH BRAISED CABBAGE AND APPLE

SERVES 4

Ling cod is a delicious west coast fish that is not actually in the cod family. Its firm, white flesh makes it popular with chefs, not to mention it's a sustainable seafood choice. Here, the bright white flesh is stunning set on top of deep purple cabbage. For an elegant dinner party, serve this after Shaved Fennel and Crab Salad (page 54).

1. To make the Braised Cabbage, heat the olive oil in a medium saucepan over medium heat. Add the garlic and cook, stirring, for 1 minute. Reduce the heat to medium-low and stir in the cabbage. Cover and cook, stirring frequently, until the cabbage begins to soften, about 10 minutes.

2. Add the rice vinegar and thyme, and season with salt and pepper. Cover and continue to cook for 15 minutes.

3. Add the apple and butter; stir well. Cover and keep warm.

4. Preheat the oven to 400°F (200°C). Line a baking sheet with parchment paper.

5. Place the cod fillets on the baking sheet and top with butter. Squeeze the lemon wedges over the fish and arrange the lemon sections around the fish. Season with salt and pepper. Bake for 15 minutes, or until the fish begins to flake.

6. Divide the braised cabbage among 4 plates, making a bed for the fish. Carefully remove the cod from the baking sheet and serve it on the braised cabbage.

Braised Cabbage

3 tablespoons (45 mL) olive oil
1 clove garlic, minced
1 head purple cabbage, cored and shredded
3 tablespoons (45 mL) unseasoned rice vinegar
1 tablespoon (15 mL) chopped fresh thyme
Kosher salt and freshly ground pepper
1 apple, cored and chopped
3 tablespoons (45 mL) unsalted butter

For the Ling Cod

4 ling cod fillets (6 ounces/170 g each)
3 tablespoons (45 mL) unsalted butter, softened
1 lemon, cut into 6 wedges

CAMPFIRE-STYLE RAINBOW TROUT

SERVES 4

We've learned over time not to grill fish directly on barbecue grates. The best way to cook fish outdoors is in a cast-iron pan on the grill. No more burnt fish from flare-ups or skin torn on grates. Just crispy skin, moist meat, and the fresh air! To guarantee crispy skin, the skin must be dried off very well before cooking, and the pan must be very hot before the fish is added. We love fresh trout in this recipe, but you can also use sockeye salmon, yellow perch, or even shrimp. You can garnish this fish with Salsa Verde (page 257). An excellent appetizer would be Green Beans with Miso Dressing (page 75).

---

4 whole fresh rainbow trout (1½ pounds/
 675 g each), scaled
6 lemon slices, cut in half
Fresh thyme sprigs
Fresh rosemary sprigs
Salt and freshly ground pepper
4 tablespoons (60 mL) olive oil, divided

1. Preheat a grill to high.

2. Rinse the fish well under cold running water, running your finger up the cavity to clean it out. Drain well and pat dry with plenty of paper towels. (This is important for crispy skin.) Neatly stuff each cavity with lemon slices, thyme, and rosemary. Sprinkle cavities with salt and pepper. Brush the fish all over with 2 tablespoons (30 mL) of the olive oil.

3. Heat a large cast-iron skillet over the hot grill. Add the remaining 2 tablespoons (30 mL) olive oil. When the oil is hot, gently place the fish in the pan, making sure they don't touch each other. (Cook in batches if needed.) Cook for 4 minutes per side, or until the skin is crispy and the flesh flakes easily. The internal temperature should reach 135°F (58°C).

4. Carefully remove the fish from the pan and let it rest for about 5 minutes before serving.

CRAB CAKES WITH CITRUS CHUTNEY

MAKES 12 CRAB CAKES; SERVES 4

These beautiful crab cakes are an absolute splurge. Make them when you can get fresh crabmeat from a fishmonger. Go ahead and reward yourself and the ones you love. Be gentle when shaping the cakes—better to have very loose and tender crab cakes than well-formed but dense ones. You will have leftover citrus chutney, which can be used on buttered toast or served with roast chicken. These cakes go well with our Heirloom Tomato Salad (page 58).

1. To make the Citrus Chutney, wash the citrus well under warm running water. Cut the lemon, orange, and limes into ⅛-inch (3 mm) rounds. Pluck out any seeds. Place the citrus in a large saucepan. Add the red pepper, brown sugar, chili flakes, and just enough water to cover. Bring to a boil over medium-high heat. Reduce the heat and simmer until the citrus peels are very soft, about 30 minutes. Add a little water if the mixture starts to dry out.

2. Cool to room temperature before serving. (The chutney keeps in the refrigerator, in a resealable container, for up to 1 month.)

3. To make the Crab Cakes, in a medium bowl, beat the egg. Add the crab, poblano chili, cilantro, garlic, lime zest, Basic Mayonnaise, mustard, Lawry's Seasoned Salt, and cayenne. Mix well to combine, but do not overwork the mixture—try to keep it airy.

4. Divide the mixture into 12 equal portions. Shape them into hamburger-like patties. Dredge them lightly in the panko crumbs.

5. Heat ¼ cup (60 mL) of the canola oil in a non-stick skillet over medium heat. Working in batches, fry the Crab Cakes for 2 to 3 minutes on each side, or until golden brown, using the remaining ¼ cup (60 mL) canola oil as needed. Drain the Crab Cakes on a plate lined with paper towel. Serve hot with the Citrus Chutney.

Citrus Chutney (makes 2 cups/500 mL)
1 lemon, ends trimmed (or 2 Meyer lemons)
1 orange, ends trimmed
2 limes, ends trimmed
1 sweet red pepper, seeded and diced
2 cups (500 mL) lightly packed brown sugar
½ teaspoon (2 mL) red chili flakes

Crab Cakes
1 large egg
1¼ pounds (565 g) fresh crabmeat, picked over
¼ cup (60 mL) minced poblano chili
2 tablespoons (30 mL) minced fresh cilantro
1 clove garlic, minced
Grated zest of 1 lime
1 cup (250 mL) Basic Mayonnaise (page 246) or store-bought
¼ cup (60 mL) Dijon mustard
½ teaspoon (2 mL) Lawry's Seasoned Salt or Old Bay seasoning
¼ teaspoon (1 mL) cayenne pepper
1 cup (250 mL) panko crumbs
½ cup (125 mL) canola oil, divided

ROASTED SALMON AND SEAWEED RICE BOWLS

Simply set out all these components in individual plates or bowls and allow everyone to put together their own meal. Works well with picky eaters and fussy kids. Seaweed has become very popular lately, making its way into cookies, crackers, and even dried pasta. We hope to introduce you to the real stuff here. Seaweed is high in vitamins, minerals, and nutrients, and deserves its status as a superfood. We love the complex flavours and textures it adds to our dishes.

---

1 whole side of wild red spring or sockeye salmon with skin (1½ pounds/675 g), pin bones removed

3 tablespoons (45 mL) canola oil

3 tablespoons (45 mL) Umami Sauce (page 264), for garnish

1 tablespoon (15 mL) fresh chives cut into ½-inch (1 cm) pieces, for garnish

1 tablespoon (15 mL) black sesame seeds, for garnish

2 cups (500 mL) shelled edamame, cooked in salted water until tender

2 cups (500 mL) Roasted Mushrooms (page 150)

2 cups (500 mL) peeled and grated carrots

¼ cup (60 mL) dried arame seaweed, soaked in boiling water for 5 minutes, drained

½ cup (125 mL) dried dulse seaweed, dipped in cold water for 2 minutes, cut into 1-inch (2.5 cm) pieces

¼ cup (60 mL) dried wakame seaweed, soaked in water for 10 minutes, drained

¼ cup (60 mL) Miso Dressing (page 245)

2 cups (500 mL) cooked sushi rice

1. To cook the salmon, preheat the oven to 400°F (200°C).

2. Heat the canola oil in a large, heavy skillet over medium-high heat. When the oil is hot, place the salmon in the skillet, skin side down, and cook for 5 minutes. Transfer to the oven and roast for 15 minutes, or until the skin is well seared and the internal temperature has reached 135°F (58°C). Let rest on a platter for at least 10 minutes before serving. Garnish with Umami Sauce, chives, and sesame seeds.

3. Lightly dress the edamame, Roasted Mushrooms, carrots, arame, dulse, and wakame with the Miso Dressing and place them in separate serving bowls. Allow your guests to choose which combination they want to put on their rice.

ROASTED SWORDFISH WITH UMAMI SAUCE

SERVES 4

This dish is all about the beauty of a fresh swordfish steak. A very light pan sauce of citrus and a slight crust makes this dish a flavour bomb. Don't be heavy handed with the crust—as with all fresh fish, less is more. Serve on a bed of steamed rice with a side of Green Beans with Miso Dressing (page 75) or Roasted Eggplant with Miso and Green Peppers (page 73).

1. Preheat the oven to 400°F (200°C). Line a baking sheet with parchment paper.

2. Combine the sesame seeds and hazelnuts. Spread them on a plate.

3. Season the swordfish with salt and pepper and brush all over with 2 tablespoons (30 mL) of the Umami Sauce to help the seeds stick to the fish. Firmly press the fish into the seed mixture to coat all sides. Place the fish on the lined baking sheet.

4. Roast for 18 minutes, or until a thin knife meets little resistance at the steak's thickest point.

5. While the fish roasts, in a small saucepan, bring the orange juice to a boil over medium-high heat. Add the ginger and the remaining 2 tablespoons (30 mL) Umami Sauce. Boil, stirring frequently, for 4 minutes. Remove from the heat and whisk in the butter until the sauce is smooth. Pour the sauce over the fish and serve immediately.

1 cup (250 mL) sesame seeds
1 tablespoon (15 mL) ground hazelnuts
4 swordfish steaks (7 ounces/200 g each)
Kosher salt and freshly ground pepper
4 tablespoons (60 mL) Umami Sauce (page 264), divided
¼ cup (60 mL) freshly squeezed orange juice
1 tablespoon (15 mL) minced fresh ginger
3 tablespoons (45 mL) unsalted butter

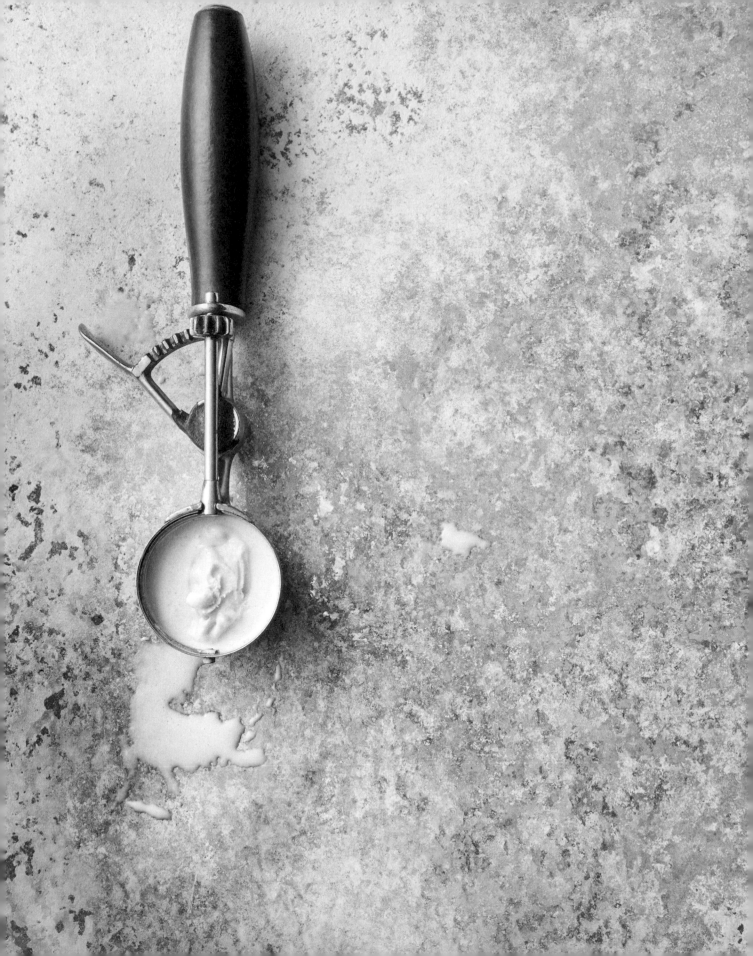

PASTRY AND DESSERTS

COCONUT CRANBERRY GRANOLA

MAKES 6 CUPS (1.5 L)

We developed this recipe quite early on. Like many items we offer, this one is tried and true. We use this granola in yogurt parfaits topped with fresh berries and drizzled with honey; add it to cookies, muffins, and breakfast cereal; and have started to add it to savoury salads. Try it on the Squash and Apple Salad (page 53).

1. Preheat the oven to 350°F (180°C). Line a baking sheet with parchment paper.

2. On the prepared baking sheet, combine the rolled oats, sunflower seeds, pumpkin seeds, pecans, almonds, and 6 tablespoons (90 mL) of the coconut.

3. In a small pot, combine the honey, canola oil, maple syrup, cinnamon, vanilla, and salt. Bring to a boil, stirring. Pour the honey mixture over the granola mixture and, with a spoon, mix together to coat everything evenly.

4. Bake until golden brown, about 15 minutes, rotating the baking sheet once and stirring the granola a few times so it evenly browns.

5. Remove from the oven and stir in the currants, cranberries, and the remaining 6 tablespoons (90 mL) coconut. Let cool completely. Store in an airtight container for up to 2 weeks.

4 cups (1 L) old-fashioned rolled oats
⅓ cup (75 mL) raw sunflower seeds
⅓ cup (75 mL) raw pumpkin seeds
⅓ cup (75 mL) raw pecans, chopped
⅓ cup (75 mL) raw almonds, chopped
¾ cup (175 mL) sweetened shredded coconut, divided
⅓ cup (75 mL) liquid honey
⅓ cup (75 mL) canola oil
4 teaspoons (20 mL) pure maple syrup
1 teaspoon (5 mL) cinnamon
1 teaspoon (5 mL) pure vanilla extract
½ teaspoon (2 mL) kosher salt
½ cup (125 mL) currants
¼ cup (60 mL) dried cranberries

NED'S POWER COOKIES

Our good friend chef Ned Bell developed this recipe when he was the executive chef at the Four Seasons Hotel in Vancouver. We thought our customers would appreciate some healthy baked goods, and his power cookies fit the bill. Ned's cookies are a big hit.

2½ cups (625 mL) old-fashioned rolled oats

2 cups (500 mL) quinoa flour

1¾ cups (425 mL) mini dark chocolate chips

1¼ cups (300 mL) dried cranberries

1 cup (250 mL) lightly packed brown sugar

1 cup (250 mL) raw sunflower seeds

¾ cup + 2 tablespoons (205 mL) raw pumpkin seeds

½ cup (125 mL) sweetened shredded coconut

¼ cup (60 mL) flax seeds

1 tablespoon (15 mL) cinnamon

2½ teaspoons (12 mL) kosher salt

1 cup (250 mL) non-dairy milk (almond, rice, or soy milk)

¾ cup (175 mL) canola oil

¼ cup (60 mL) fancy molasses

¼ cup (60 mL) water

1. Put the oven racks in the upper and lower thirds of the oven and preheat the oven to 350°F (180°C). Line 2 baking sheets with parchment paper.

2. In the bowl of a stand mixer fitted with the paddle attachment, combine the rolled oats, quinoa flour, chocolate chips, cranberries, brown sugar, sunflower seeds, pumpkin seeds, coconut, flax seeds, cinnamon, and salt. Mix on medium speed until well combined.

3. In a medium bowl, whisk together the milk, canola oil, molasses, and water. Add the wet mixture to the dry mixture and mix on low speed until thoroughly combined.

4. Using a ⅓-cup (75 mL) measuring cup, place 12 scoops of dough on each baking sheet. With wet hands, press each dough ball down to about ½-inch (1 cm) thickness. For even baking, rotate the sheets front to back and top to bottom halfway through. These cookies do not spread during baking. Bake for 15 to 18 minutes, until slightly brown and fragrant. Transfer to wire racks and let cool completely. Store in an airtight container for up to 3 days.

APPLE CIDER MUFFINS 2.0

MAKES 12 MUFFINS

A perennial favourite recipe that's similar to one in our first cookbook, *Earth to Table*.
Erin, our pastry chef, has tweaked this recipe over the years, hence the version 2.0.

1. Preheat the oven to 350°F (180°C). Line a muffin tin with 12 paper liners.

2. In the bowl of a stand mixer fitted with the whisk attachment, combine the brown sugar, white sugar, canola oil, and eggs. Whisk until well blended.

3. Add the apple cider, sour cream, and vanilla. Whisk until combined.

4. Add the flour, baking soda, cinnamon, and salt. Whisk until thoroughly combined.

5. Divide the batter evenly among the muffin liners, filling approximately three-quarters full. Bake until puffed and golden brown, 20 to 25 minutes, rotating the tin halfway through. Tip the muffins out of the tin and cool on a rack. Store in an airtight container for up to 3 days.

1¼ cups (300 mL) lightly packed brown sugar
1 cup (250 mL) white sugar
¾ cup (175 mL) canola oil
3 large eggs
1 cup (250 mL) dry apple cider
¾ cup (175 mL) sour cream
1 teaspoon (5 mL) pure vanilla extract
2¾ cups (675 mL) all-purpose flour
1½ teaspoons (7 mL) baking soda
1½ teaspoons (7 mL) cinnamon
½ teaspoon (2 mL) kosher salt

BREAD PUDDING

SERVES 8

This bread pudding cannot come off our menu, it's that good. Trust us, one bite will immediately erase any memory of bad, gloppy bread pudding. One thing that makes Bread Bar's bread pudding stand out from the rest is that we stuff it full of day-old croissants, broken cookies, and brownie trim. You can too! At the restaurants we serve our bread pudding warm, topped with cappuccino ice cream and white chocolate sauce.

1 loaf day-old white bread
1½ cups (375 mL) whole milk
1½ cups (375 mL) heavy (35%) cream
3 large eggs
5 large egg yolks
½ cup (125 mL) + 2 tablespoons (30 mL) sugar, divided
⅛ teaspoon (0.5 mL) kosher salt

1. Preheat the oven to 325°F (160°C). Grease an 11- x 7-inch (2 L) baking dish with unsalted butter and dust with sugar. Tap out the excess sugar.

2. Cut the bread into 1-inch (2.5 cm) slices, then cut each slice into 6 pieces. Scatter them into the baking dish. The bread should provide just the right amount of cubes to fill the baking dish. Set aside.

3. To prepare the custard, in a medium saucepan, bring the milk and cream to a boil, then remove from the heat.

4. Whisk the eggs and egg yolks in a large bowl until blended. Add ½ cup (125 mL) of the sugar and the salt and whisk until blended. Slowly add the hot milk mixture to the eggs, whisking constantly to ensure the eggs don't curdle.

5. Pour the custard over the bread. Press down on the bread every now and then to make sure each cube soaks up the custard. The baking dish should be about three-quarters full and the bread exposed above the custard. Cover the baking dish with parchment paper and then cover tightly with foil.

6. Place the baking dish in a large roasting pan and add enough hot water to come halfway up the side of the baking dish. Carefully transfer to the oven and bake for 45 minutes to 1 hour, or until the pudding is springy and set, not wet and runny—a knife will come out clean. Remove from the oven, but leave the oven on. Remove the baking dish from the water bath and remove the foil and parchment paper.

7. Sprinkle the bread pudding with the remaining 2 tablespoons (30 mL) sugar and return to the oven to brown, about 10 minutes. Cool on a rack for at least 30 minutes, then serve warm. Store, covered and refrigerated, for up to 5 days.

MONKEY BREAD

MAKES 12 MONKEY BREADS •
REQUIRES TIME FOR PREP

Tiny brioche balls, coated in cinnamon sugar, baked in a bundle, and drizzled with frosting while still warm—what's not to love? Kids drag their parents to our pastry counter for two things: chocolate cookies and Monkey Bread. We love to see their eyes light up (and not just the kids'!) when they discover that there is Monkey Bread to be had. We have sometimes topped these confections with candied nuts or seasonal fruit jams, but honestly, less is more.

Brioche

4⅔ cups (1.15 L) all-purpose flour

¼ cup + 2 tablespoons (90 mL) sugar

1 tablespoon (15 mL) kosher salt

2 tablespoons (30 mL) instant dry yeast

4 large eggs

2 large egg yolks

1 cup (250 mL) warm water

2 cups (500 mL) unsalted butter, cubed, softened

Cinnamon Sugar

1 cup (250 mL) sugar

¼ cup (60 mL) cinnamon

Glaze

1 cup (250 mL) icing sugar

½ cup (125 mL) heavy (35%) cream

1. To make the Brioche, in a stand mixer fitted with the dough hook, combine the flour, sugar, salt, and yeast. Mix at medium speed until combined.

2. Add the eggs, egg yolks, and water and mix on medium speed until well combined. Turn the speed up one level and beat until a smooth, soft, and elastic dough forms, about 10 minutes. Do the stretch test: pinch some of the dough and pull it upward. If the dough feels springy and elastic, it is ready.

3. Add the butter one piece at a time, mixing well after each addition, and making sure to scrape down the sides and bottom of the bowl. Eventually the dough will come away from the sides of the bowl in a smooth mass.

4. Transfer the dough to a lightly buttered large bowl, cover with plastic wrap, and refrigerate for 24 hours.

5. Remove the dough from the refrigerator and let it come to room temperature, about 1 hour. Punch down the dough and flip it over in the bowl, completely deflating it. (At this point the dough can be wrapped in plastic wrap and frozen for up to 1 month.)

6. To make the Cinnamon Sugar, stir together the sugar and cinnamon in a small bowl.

7. Line a muffin tin with 12 paper liners. Pinch off small pieces from the dough (you will want 36 pieces altogether) and roll each one between your palms into a ½-inch (1 cm) ball. Roll the balls in the Cinnamon Sugar. Snugly place 3 dough balls into each muffin liner. Cover the muffin tin with a kitchen towel and let the dough rise in a warm spot in the kitchen for 1 hour, or until doubled in size.

8. Meanwhile, preheat the oven to 350°F (180°C).

9. Remove the kitchen towel and bake the breads for 20 minutes, or until golden. Let cool slightly in the tin. Glaze the Monkey Bread while it is still slightly warm.

10. To make the Glaze, combine the icing sugar and cream in a small bowl and blend with a fork until smooth.

11. Drizzle the Monkey Bread with the Glaze and serve. Best served the day it is made.

BLUEBERRY SCONES

MAKES 6 LARGE SCONES • REQUIRES TIME FOR PREP

These scones are so decadent that some of our customers plan their entire day around eating one. They are delicate and have a crispy sugary crust. We have them on the counter every day, but on the weekends we have to bake twice as many. Blueberry white chocolate is the flavour we share here, but we also make raspberry milk chocolate, mixed berry with white chocolate, and in the spring, rhubarb with ginger.

1. Preheat the oven to 350°F (180°C). Line a baking sheet with parchment paper.

2. In a large bowl, combine the sugar and lemon zest and rub between your hands until fragrant. Add the flour, baking powder, baking soda, and salt; mix until combined.

3. Add the shortening and butter and massage them in with your fingers until the mixture resembles coarse crumbs. Add the chocolate and lightly toss.

4. Add 1 cup (250 mL) of the cream and mix with your hands until barely combined. Add the blueberries and continue mixing with your hands just until you have a soft, ragged dough that stays together and no dry bits of flour are left on the bottom of the bowl. Do not overwork the dough or the scones will be tough. Cover and refrigerate until chilled, about 1 hour.

5. Tip the dough out onto a well-floured work surface. Roll out the dough into a disc that is 1 inch (2.5 cm) thick, then cut it into six 3-inch (8 cm) triangles. Place the scones on the prepared baking sheet, evenly spaced. Brush the tops with the remaining ¼ cup (60 mL) cream and dust with a generous sprinkle of sugar.

6. Bake for 20 minutes, or until golden brown, rotating the baking sheet halfway through. Transfer scones to a rack and cool.

¾ cup (175 mL) sugar, plus more for topping
1 teaspoon (5 mL) grated lemon zest
4 cups (1 L) all-purpose flour
1 tablespoon (15 mL) baking powder
1 teaspoon (5 mL) baking soda
1 teaspoon (5 mL) salt
⅔ cup (150 mL) shortening, cut into large pieces
⅔ cup (150 mL) unsalted butter, cut into large pieces, softened
1 cup (250 mL) white chocolate chips or shavings
1¼ cups (300 mL) heavy (35%) cream, divided
1 cup (250 mL) fresh or frozen (not thawed) blueberries

BUTTERMILK BISCUITS

MAKES 9 OR 10 BISCUITS • REQUIRES TIME FOR PREP

In the American south, where biscuits are revered, recipes vary from region to region, if not family to family. We would put these biscuits up for judging at any county fair east of the Mississippi. Our secret is grating the butter on a box grater, which keeps the butter cold and ensures a tender biscuit. (Shown on page 170.)

3½ cups (875 mL) all-purpose flour

2 tablespoons + 2 teaspoons (40 mL) baking powder

1 tablespoon (15 mL) kosher salt

4 teaspoons (20 mL) fresh thyme leaves

1 cup (250 mL) cold unsalted butter

2 cups (500 mL) buttermilk, plus more to brush the biscuits

1. In a medium bowl, combine the flour, baking powder, salt, and thyme. Stir together with your hands. Using the large holes of a box grater, grate the cold butter into the flour mixture; toss well with your hands. While mixing with your hand, add the buttermilk in a thin stream until dough just comes together. (You may not use all the buttermilk.)

2. Tip the dough out onto a lightly floured work surface. Roll out the dough into a rectangle ½ inch (1 cm) thick, pressing down with your hands if bits begin to crumble off. Be firm with the dough, but press on it rather than knead it.

3. Cut the dough in half crosswise, and carefully stack one half on top of the other. Gently roll out again into a rectangle ½ inch (1 cm) thick. (This stacking process creates layers that will make your biscuits crumbly and light.) Cut and stack as before, then roll out into a rectangle ¾ inch (2 cm) thick.

4. Line a baking sheet with parchment paper. Cut the dough into biscuits (squares, triangles, or circles), place the biscuits on the baking sheet, and chill in the fridge for 30 minutes.

5. Meanwhile, preheat the oven to 350°F (180°C).

6. Brush the tops of the biscuits with buttermilk. Bake for 18 to 20 minutes, or until puffed and golden brown, rotating the baking sheet halfway through. Transfer biscuits to a rack to cool.

TOFFEE BITS

MAKES 2 CUPS (500 ML)

We make these bits to serve atop our Chocolate Brownies (page 220). Pair them up with something chocolate and Salted Caramel Sauce (page 219, below) for a magic match. Toffee Bits can also be used in cookie dough or sprinkled on ice cream. (Shown on page 221.)

1. Line a baking sheet with parchment paper.

2. In a medium saucepan, combine the butter, sugar, water, corn syrup, and salt. Bring to a boil over high heat and cook until a candy thermometer registers 280°F (138°C). Stir to even out the colour. Remove from the heat and carefully pour the toffee onto the prepared baking sheet. Let cool to room temperature.

3. Break the toffee into large pieces, and in a food processor, blitz into bits. Store in an airtight container for up to 2 weeks.

½ cup (125 mL) unsalted butter
¾ cup (175 mL) sugar
2 tablespoons (30 mL) water
1 tablespoon (15 mL) corn syrup
½ teaspoon (2 mL) kosher salt

SALTED CARAMEL SAUCE

MAKES 2 CUPS (500 ML)

We serve the rich, creamy sauce atop our Chocolate Brownies (page 220). It is also fun to use in the fall as a dip for apples and pears. Adding lemon juice to the sugar will stop the caramel from crystallizing and save you from having to brush down the sides of the pan with water. This sauce becomes quite solid once it has cooled in the refrigerator. One minute in the microwave on medium power will make it pourable again.

1. In a medium saucepan, combine the sugar, water, and lemon juice. Bring to a rolling boil over high heat. Reduce to medium heat and cook, without stirring but occasionally swirling the pan for even cooking, until the syrup is a deep reddish brown, about 8 minutes. Remove from the heat.

2. Carefully and slowly, stir in the butter and cream. The sauce will bubble up but quickly subside. Stir in the salt.

3. Use immediately or let cool, then cover and refrigerate for up to 1 week.

2 cups (500 mL) sugar
1½ cups (375 mL) water
1 teaspoon (5 mL) freshly squeezed lemon juice
¼ cup (60 mL) unsalted butter, cubed
1 cup (250 mL) heavy (35%) cream
¼ cup (60 mL) flaky sea salt (we use Maldon)

CHOCOLATE BROWNIES

MAKES 12 BROWNIES

Out of all the desserts we serve, this is one we can't take off the menu or there would be a community mutiny. This brownie is our most chocolaty dish, and who does not have a love affair with chocolate? We serve our brownies warm, topped with Salted Caramel Sauce (page 219), Toffee Bits (page 219), and organic vanilla ice cream—which only adds to the brownie's popularity.

10 ounces (280 g) high-quality semi-sweet chocolate (we use Lindt), chopped

1 cup (250 mL) unsalted butter

1¼ cups (300 mL) all-purpose flour

3 tablespoons (45 mL) high-quality cocoa powder (we use Lindt)

1 teaspoon (5 mL) kosher salt

4 large eggs

2⅔ cups (650 mL) sugar

2 teaspoons (10 mL) pure vanilla extract

1. Preheat the oven to 350°F (180°C). Line a 13- x 9-inch (3.5 L) baking pan with parchment paper, extending the paper up the sides of the pan.

2. In a large saucepan, bring an inch or so of water to a simmer over low heat. Combine the chocolate and butter in a medium heatproof bowl and set the bowl over the pan. Stir the chocolate mixture occasionally until it is almost all melted. Remove from the heat and stir until the mixture is completely melted and smooth. Set aside.

3. In a medium bowl, whisk together the flour, cocoa powder, and salt.

4. In a large bowl, using an electric mixer, beat the eggs with the sugar and vanilla until the mixture is thickened and pale, about 2 minutes. Pour the warm chocolate mixture into the egg mixture, stirring to blend well. Add the flour mixture. Using a rubber spatula, fold it in until well combined.

5. Pour the batter into the prepared pan and bake for 35 minutes, or until set—the surface will be dry and have a few cracks. Rotate the pan halfway through. Don't overcook these brownies, as gooeyness is what we are going for. Let the brownies cool completely in the pan before lifting them out and cutting.

COCONUT MACAROONS

MAKES 6 MACAROONS

Every day customers ask us what our gluten-free options are. These delicious macaroons are naturally gluten-free and are a treat enjoyed by everyone.

1. Preheat the oven to 325°F (160°C). Line a baking sheet with parchment paper.

2. In a medium bowl, whisk together the egg whites, sugar, vanilla, and salt until frothy. Add the coconut and mix until evenly coated.

3. Form the coconut mixture into 6 golf-ball-size balls with your hands or an ice cream scoop and arrange on the lined baking sheet. Bake until golden brown, 10 to 12 minutes, rotating the baking sheet halfway through.

4. Let the macaroons cool on the baking sheet for 5 minutes, then transfer to a wire rack to cool completely. Once cooled drizzle with chocolate sauce. Store in an airtight container for up to 1 week.

3 egg whites
½ cup (125 mL) sugar
1 teaspoon (5 mL) pure vanilla extract
½ teaspoon (2 mL) kosher salt
4 cups (1 L) sweetened shredded coconut
Chocolate sauce, for topping

LEMON SQUARES

MAKES TWELVE 3-INCH (8 CM) SQUARES •
REQUIRES TIME FOR PREP

The burst of lemon flavour in this
customer favourite comes from the oils
in the zested peel and from the juice.
In the fall we serve these squares
topped with meringue that has been
browned with a kitchen torch.

Lemon Filling
2¼ cups (550 mL) sugar
Grated zest of 1 lemon
½ cup (125 mL) all-purpose flour
1 cup + 2 tablespoons (280 mL) freshly
   squeezed lemon juice
6 large eggs
1 large egg yolk
¼ teaspoon (1 mL) kosher salt

Crust
¾ cup (175 mL) unsalted butter, softened
½ cup (125 mL) icing sugar
1½ cups (375 mL) all-purpose flour

1. To make the Lemon Filling, in a medium bowl, combine the sugar and lemon zest and rub well between your hands. This will bring out the fragrant oils. Add the flour and whisk with a fork until combined. Slowly add the lemon juice, whisking constantly with the fork until a smooth paste forms.

2. In another medium bowl, whisk together the eggs, egg yolk, and salt. Add the egg mixture to the sugar mixture and, using a whisk, whip until smooth. Cover the bowl with plastic wrap and let the filling sit in the refrigerator overnight.

3. To make the crust, in a stand mixer fitted with the paddle attachment, beat the butter with the icing sugar on high speed until very light and fluffy, about 5 minutes. Add the flour and mix until combined. Shape the dough into a disc, wrap tightly with plastic wrap, and chill for at least 1 hour.

4. Line a 13- x 9-inch (3.5 L) baking pan with parchment paper, extending the paper up the sides of the pan. Pinch off chunks of the chilled dough and, with your fingers, firmly and evenly press the dough into the bottom and up the sides of the pan, bringing it up to the rim of the pan. Make sure the crust is an even thickness over the entire pan. Prick the bottom all over with a fork, cover, and chill for 1 hour.

5. Meanwhile, preheat the oven to 350°F (180°C).

6. Using a spoon, skim the froth off the top of the filling and discard it.

7. Bake the crust for 10 to 15 minutes, or until golden brown. Remove from the oven. Reduce the oven to 300°F (150°C).

8. Pour about 1 cup (250 mL) of the filling over the crust and tip the pan so the filling covers the bottom and seals any cracks. Bake for 5 minutes. Pour in the remaining filling and bake until just barely set, 15 to 20 minutes.

9. Let cool completely on a rack. These squares are best served the day they are made, but any leftovers can be covered and refrigerated for up to 3 days.

BUTTER TARTS

Butter tarts are quintessential Canadian pastries, though there are many international relatives, like pecan pie, treacle tart, and shoofly pie. We are butter tart purists: no nuts, no raisins, no fancy additions. In our world, this is the perfect butter tart. If you insist on breaking what is not broken, we suggest adding a couple of tablespoons of cooked chopped bacon to the filling and drizzling with maple syrup. Deliciously Canadian!

1. To make the dough, in a food processor, combine the flour, sugar, and salt. Pulse three times to mix. Add the butter and pulse in short bursts until the mixture resembles coarse crumbs. Add the water and, using long pulses, process until the dough comes together. Stop the machine and feel the dough. It should hold together well when squeezed. Add a little more water if the mixture is too dry. Press into a disc, wrap in plastic wrap, and refrigerate until chilled, about 1 hour.

2. Preheat the oven to 350°F (180°C). Spray a muffin tin with non-stick baking spray.

3. To make the filling, in a medium bowl, whisk together the eggs, brown sugar, corn syrup, butter, vanilla, and salt until blended. Set aside.

4. On a lightly floured work surface, roll out the dough until ⅛ inch (3 mm) thick. Using a 5-inch (12 cm) round cookie cutter, cut out 12 circles, rerolling scraps if necessary. Line the muffin tin with the dough circles.

5. Using a spoon, divide the filling evenly among the tarts, filling each one approximately three-quarters full. Bake for 20 minutes, or until the pastry is golden and the filling is puffed and golden brown. Let rest for a few minutes on a rack, then run a thin knife around the edges of the tarts anywhere the filling has run down the side. Let stand for another 5 minutes so the tarts firm up, then use a thin offset spatula to transfer them to a rack to cool completely. Store in an airtight container for up to 3 days.

Dough
2 cups (500 mL) all-purpose flour
2 teaspoons (10 mL) sugar
1 teaspoon (5 mL) kosher salt
1 cup (250 mL) cold unsalted butter, cubed
¼ cup (60 mL) cold water

Filling
2 large eggs
½ cup (125 mL) lightly packed brown sugar
½ cup (125 mL) corn syrup
¼ cup (60 mL) unsalted butter, melted
1 teaspoon (5 mL) pure vanilla extract
Pinch of kosher salt

RHUBARB UPSIDE-DOWN CAKE

MAKES ONE 9-INCH (23 CM) ROUND CAKE

We had a version of this cake in our first cookbook, *Earth to Table*, baked with blueberries and with a much denser cornmeal crust. This is a preferred lighter version. Rhubarb is easy to grow and a nice, sturdy plant that returns each year, signalling spring. We love how easily this cake comes together, and how easily it can accommodate whatever fruit comes from our farm—or your market.

Crumble Topping

½ cup (125 mL) all-purpose flour
¼ cup (60 mL) sugar
¼ teaspoon (1 mL) kosher salt
4 tablespoons (60 mL) unsalted butter, melted

Rhubarb Cake

1 pound (450 g) fresh rhubarb stalks, each cut into 5 pieces
1¾ cups (425 mL) sugar
Grated zest and juice of 1 medium orange
¾ cup (175 mL) unsalted butter, softened
2 large eggs
1½ cups (375 mL) all-purpose flour
1½ teaspoons (7 mL) baking powder
1½ teaspoons (7 mL) kosher salt
1 cup (250 mL) full-fat sour cream

Toppings

Pure maple syrup
Whipped cream

1. Preheat the oven to 350°F (180°C). Grease a 9-inch (23 cm) cake pan and line the bottom with parchment paper.

2. To make the Crumble Topping, in a small bowl, combine the flour, sugar, salt, and butter. Work together with a fork to form coarse crumbs. Set aside.

3. To make the Rhubarb Cake, in a medium bowl, combine the rhubarb and ¼ cup (60 mL) of the sugar; toss to coat. Set aside.

4. In a stand mixer fitted with the paddle attachment, combine the remaining 1½ cups (375 mL) sugar and the orange zest; beat on medium speed until fragrant. Carefully add the butter and beat on high speed until light and fluffy, about 5 minutes, scraping down the sides of the bowl intermittently. Add the orange juice and eggs. Mix on medium-low speed, occasionally scraping down the sides of the bowl, until fully incorporated.

5. In a medium bowl, whisk together the flour, baking powder, and salt. Add to the batter and mix on medium speed until just combined. Add the sour cream and mix until just combined. Overmixing will toughen the cake.

6. Arrange the rhubarb pieces in an even layer in the bottom of the cake pan. Pour over any juices in the bowl. Dollop the cake batter over the rhubarb and spread evenly with the back of a wet spoon. Sprinkle the Crumble Topping evenly over the top.

7. Bake until golden brown and a cake tester comes out clean, about 45 minutes. Let cool for 15 minutes, then run a knife around the edge of the cake pan. Invert a cake plate over the pan and, using oven mitts, turn the pan upside down to flip the cake onto the plate. Remove the parchment paper.

8. Serve warm with a drizzle of maple syrup and dollop of whipped cream.

BASIC PIE DOUGH

MAKES TWO 10-INCH (25 CM) PIE SHELLS • REQUIRES TIME FOR PREP

Pies are in our DNA. Over the years we have made about a million pies. Early on we determined that a crumble top was our preference rather than a crust top. We also discovered that this is a real area of debate within the pie-making world! But the added flavours of a crumble top prevailed, and that's what you'll find at Bread Bar. The secret to a good pie dough (besides good ingredients and not overworking the dough) is to give it time to rest before rolling it out. If you have ever had problems with your pie dough shrinking, it is because the dough has not had time to relax.

---

1. In a food processor, combine the flour, sugar, salt, and shortening and pulse until the mixture resembles a coarse meal. There should be pebbles of shortening throughout the mixture.

2. While using long pulses, add the ice water and pulse until the dough comes together. Squeeze a clump of dough in your hand. If it does not hold together, add a little more water and stir or pulse, then check again. Repeat as necessary.

3. Turn the dough out onto a lightly floured work surface and gather it into a rough ball. You want to be careful not to overwork the dough and not to add too much flour. Cut the ball in half with a knife. Using the heel of your hand, flatten each portion of dough once or twice, then knead each piece back into a ball.

4. Flatten each ball into a 5-inch (12 cm) disc and dust lightly with flour. Tightly wrap in plastic wrap and refrigerate for at least 1 hour.

5. On a liberally floured work surface, roll out one disc of dough into a circle about 11 inches (28 cm) across. Start rolling from the centre and work your way out in all directions. Carefully roll the dough around the rolling pin and unroll it right over the pie plate. Gently press into the pie plate, crimping the edges using the thumb and index finger of the left hand and pinching with the index finger of the right hand. Repeat with the second disc of dough.

6. Wrap the shells carefully in plastic wrap and refrigerate for at least 3 hours, though overnight is best. The pie shells may also be frozen for up to 1 month.

2 cups (500 mL) all-purpose flour
1 tablespoon (15 mL) sugar
1 teaspoon (5 mL) kosher salt
1 cup (250 mL) vegetable shortening
⅓ cup (75 mL) ice water

CHERRY PIE

We have a long history of pie making at our restaurant. Bettina started to make this pie to sell at local farmers' markets years ago, and the recipe hasn't changed over the years. It's so simple, yet probably the best-tasting pie. This pie freezes very well unbaked, and fits nicely in a resealable freezer bag. If baking from frozen, bake for 1½ hours. Serve this with Smash-In Ice Cream (page 235).

---

4 cups (1 L) fresh or frozen (not thawed) pitted sour cherries
1 Basic Pie Dough 10-inch (25 cm) pie shell (page 231)

Pie Dusting
½ cup (125 mL) lightly packed brown sugar
½ cup (125 mL) white sugar, divided
3 tablespoons (45 mL) cornstarch
1 teaspoon (5 mL) salt

Pie Crumble
1 cup (250 mL) all-purpose flour
¾ cup (175 mL) old-fashioned rolled oats
½ cup (125 mL) lightly packed brown sugar
¼ cup (60 mL) white sugar
½ teaspoon (2 mL) kosher salt
1 cup (250 mL) unsalted butter, cubed, softened

1. To make the Pie Dusting, in a small bowl, combine the brown sugar, white sugar, cornstarch, and salt; whisk together until combined. (The dusting mixture can be made ahead and stored, in an airtight container in the refrigerator, for up to 5 days.)

2. To make the Pie Crumble, in a medium bowl, combine the flour, rolled oats, brown sugar, white sugar, salt, and butter. Using your fingers, work in the butter until the mixture is combined and crumbly. (The crumble mixture can be made ahead and stored, in an airtight container in the refrigerator, for up to 5 days.)

3. Preheat the oven to 350°F (180°C).

4. Spread the cherries evenly in the prepared pie shell. Sprinkle evenly with the Pie Dusting, then top with the Pie Crumble. Bake for 1 hour. The pie is ready when the crust is golden brown and the juices are bubbling slowly. Let the pie to cool slightly before serving. The pie will keep, covered and refrigerated, for up to 2 days.

SMASH-IN ICE CREAM

This recipe grew out of our attempt to up-cycle the underused bits and pieces of pastry that may otherwise have landed in the green bin. In our first cookbook we had a smash-in recipe, encouraging readers to take leftover product—that last piece of pecan pie or that last piece of cheesecake—and smash it into ice cream. Once we opened Bread Bar, the Smash-In Ice Creams took on a life of their own. Our pastry chefs take all the bits and pieces left over from our baked goods and create delicious layered ice cream that we can't keep on the freezer shelves. At Bread Bar we can easily sell up to 60 litres a week—and in summer even more. Start with organic, quality ice cream, any flavour you choose—at Bread Bar we stick to chocolate and vanilla—and the options are limitless from there. Engage kids and your creative side, and keep us posted on your favourites.

1. Start with about 1 pint (500 mL) of ice cream, softened at room temperature for 20 minutes. Dump it into a bowl. Spread a layer of the ice cream in the bottom of the ice-cream container, then add your smash-in of choice—pictured here, clockwise from the top left: Chocolate Brownies (page 220), Lemon Squares (page 224), toasted meringue, raspberry jam, chocolate chip cookie, blackberry jam, Salted Caramel Sauce (page 219). Repeat layering ice cream and smash-in until your container is full. Freeze.

CHIPWICHES

MAKES 24 COOKIES; 12 CHIPWICHES

What makes the perfect cookie is always up for debate: soft and chewy or firm and crispy? We love soft and chewy cookies—and they work perfectly with one of our most popular desserts, the Chipwich. This is basically an ice-cream sandwich, so we need a soft cookie that will be easy to chomp down on. This is a very simple recipe, but the perfection is in the details of preparation. A well-made cookie is all in the mixing. Mix just until the flour just disappears (overmixing causes tough cookies). Use good-quality chocolate chips and you will be thrilled with the results.

1 cup (250 mL) unsalted butter, softened
1 cup (250 mL) lightly packed brown sugar
¾ cup (175 mL) white sugar
2 large eggs
2 teaspoons (10 mL) kosher salt
1 teaspoon (5 mL) baking soda
1 teaspoon (5 mL) baking powder
1 teaspoon (5 mL) pure vanilla extract
2 cups (500 mL) all-purpose flour
4 cups (1 L) semi-sweet chocolate chips, divided
Good-quality French vanilla ice cream, or your favourite flavour

1. Preheat the oven to 350°F (180°C). Line a cookie sheet with parchment paper.

2. In a stand mixer fitted with the paddle attachment, cream together the butter, brown sugar, and white sugar until light and creamy, about 5 minutes.

3. Add the eggs one at a time, beating well after each addition, and scraping down the sides of the bowl as needed. Add the salt, baking soda, baking powder, and vanilla; mix until combined. Add the flour all at once and mix until just combined.

4. Add 2 cups (500 mL) chocolate chips and stir the mixture on the lowest speed for about 30 seconds to ensure all the ingredients are evenly distributed. Make sure to mix gently so you do not knock too much air out of the cookie dough.

5. Using a ¼-cup (60 mL) measure or 2-ounce (60 mL) scoop, drop the dough onto the cookie sheet, spacing them about 3 inches (8 cm) apart. Bake for 15 minutes, or until golden brown, rotating the cookie sheet halfway through. Let cool on a wire rack for a few minutes. The cookies keep in an airtight container for up to 3 days.

6. When ready to make Chipwiches, spread the remaining 2 cups (500 mL) chocolate chips in a shallow dish. Evenly distribute a generous layer of ice cream over the flat side of one cookie; top with a second cookie, flat side down. Roll the sides of the Chipwich in the chocolate chips and enjoy immediately! Freeze any extra Chipwiches on a baking sheet, then transfer to a resealable plastic freezer bag and freeze for up to 1 month.

1. To make the Graham Crust, in a medium bowl, combine the graham cracker crumbs, brown sugar, cinnamon, and salt. Add the melted butter and stir with a fork until the butter is fully incorporated. Cover with plastic wrap and store in the refrigerator for up to 5 days.

2. To make the Cream Cheese Filling, in a stand mixer fitted with the paddle attachment, beat the cream cheese with the sugar on medium-high speed just until smooth. Scrape down the sides of the bowl. Add the vanilla and beat to incorporate.

3. Add the flour and blend on slow speed just until combined. Add the eggs and egg yolks; beat on slow speed until the eggs are fully incorporated, stopping to scrape down the sides as needed. Add the milk and beat on low speed just until blended. Cover with plastic wrap and store in the refrigerator for up to 5 days.

4. When ready to bake the cheesecake, make the Raspberry Coulis. In a small bowl, toss the raspberries with the sugar and lemon juice. Set aside for 10 to 15 minutes. The sugar will break down the raspberries. Use a fork to mash them up. You can strain out the seeds if you like, but we often leave them in.

5. Preheat the oven to 250°F (120°C). Generously spray the sides of a 10-inch (3 L) springform pan with non-stick baking spray.

6. Firmly and evenly press the graham cracker crumb mixture into the bottom of the pan, just to sides. Pour the filling over the crust. Tap the filled pan on the counter once or twice to remove any trapped air bubbles. Pour the Raspberry Coulis over the filling and use a skewer to drag the coulis around the top of the filling, creating a pattern.

7. Bake for 1½ hours, or until the centre of the cheesecake has a slight jiggle and no longer looks wet and runny. The filling will continue to cook after it's out of the oven, so don't wait for the centre to be firm. It should have a slight jiggle in the middle. Transfer to a rack and run a thin knife around the outside of the cheesecake, so it doesn't stick to the sides of the pan as it cools. Let the cheesecake cool, then refrigerate until chilled (it cuts best when chilled).

RASPBERRY SWIRL CHEESECAKE

MAKES ONE 10-INCH (25 CM) CHEESECAKE

If you have never had a cheesecake fresh from the oven, then you have not lived. For a long time this was one of Jeff's guilty pleasures. (He may have rehabilitated himself lately.) The hardest part is knowing when it's done. The centre should still have a nice jiggle when you take it out of the oven; it will continue to firm up as it cools.

Graham Crust
2 cups (500 mL) graham cracker crumbs
½ cup (125 mL) lightly packed brown sugar
1 teaspoon (5 mL) cinnamon
1 teaspoon (5 mL) kosher salt
½ cup (125 mL) unsalted butter, melted

Cream Cheese Filling
3 packages (8 ounces/250 g each) cream cheese, softened
2 cups (500 mL) sugar
1 tablespoon (15 mL) pure vanilla extract
¼ cup (60 mL) all-purpose flour
4 large eggs
2 large egg yolks
½ cup (125 mL) whole milk

Raspberry Coulis
1 cup (250 mL) fresh or thawed frozen raspberries
¼ cup (60 mL) sugar
1 teaspoon (5 mL) freshly squeezed lemon juice

STAPLES

BUTTERMILK DRESSING

MAKES 3 CUPS (750 ML)

This creamy dressing is a perfect match with our Arugula and Fennel Salad (page 49). For variation, we sometimes add chopped jalapeño peppers or fresh dill; we offer other variations below. It would also be a good dressing on our Coleslaw (page 72).

1. In a medium bowl, whisk together the Basic Mayonnaise, sour cream, and buttermilk until well blended and smooth. Season with salt and pepper.

2. Store in an airtight container, refrigerated, for up to 2 weeks.

1 cup (250 mL) Basic Mayonnaise (page 246) or store-bought
1 cup (250 mL) sour cream
1 cup (250 mL) buttermilk
Kosher salt and freshly ground pepper

Variations
1½ teaspoons (7 mL) poppy seeds
1½ teaspoons (7 mL) chopped fresh dill
1 tablespoon (15 mL) chopped jalapeño peppers
1 tablespoon (15 mL) chopped fresh chives
1 tablespoon (15 mL) grainy Dijon mustard
2 cloves Garlic Confit, mashed (page 253)
2 tablespoons (30 mL) crumbled blue cheese

HOUSE VINAIGRETTE

MAKES 1½ CUPS (375 ML)

This is our master vinaigrette. At Bread Bar we use it on almost all our salads, and on many in this cookbook, including Quinoa, Chickpea, and Black Bean Salad (page 67); Arugula and Fennel Salad (page 49); Squash and Apple Salad (page 53); Chopped Salad (page 61); French Carrot Salad (page 72); Asparagus with Green Goddess Dressing (page 76); and Taco Salad (page 79), to name just a few. We use an immersion blender to emulsify all the ingredients, resulting in a very creamy texture.

---

3 tablespoons (45 mL) chopped red onion
⅔ cup (150 mL) olive oil
¼ cup (60 mL) canola oil
¼ cup (60 mL) unseasoned rice vinegar
1 tablespoon (15 mL) sugar
1 teaspoon (5 mL) grainy Dijon mustard
Kosher salt and freshly ground pepper

1. In a blender, combine the onion, olive oil, canola oil, rice vinegar, sugar, mustard, and salt and pepper to taste. Blend until creamy, about 1 minute.

2. Store in an airtight container, refrigerated, for up to 5 days.

GREEN GODDESS DRESSING

MAKES 2 CUPS (500 ML)

This is a classic Californian recipe that adds a cool, herbaceous note to salads and pizzas. The retro name "Green Goddess" was what originally piqued our interest, and this dressing has been in constant rotation on the Bread Bar menu for years. It's right at home on any number of salads, but we have made it the star of our Asparagus with Green Goddess Dressing (page 76).

1½ cups (375 mL) Basic Mayonnaise
  (page 246) or store-bought
1 clove garlic, minced
2 white anchovies, minced (optional)
1 green onion, minced
½ cup (125 mL) fresh flat-leaf parsley,
  minced
½ cup (125 mL) fresh tarragon, minced
3 tablespoons (45 mL) minced fresh chives
2 tablespoons (30 mL) unseasoned rice
  vinegar
Kosher salt and freshly ground pepper

1. In a medium bowl, combine the Basic Mayonnaise, garlic, anchovies (if using), green onion, parsley, tarragon, chives, and rice vinegar. Whisk until well blended and smooth. Season with salt and pepper.

2. Store in an airtight container, refrigerated, for up to 2 weeks.

CAESAR SALAD DRESSING

MAKES 1½ CUPS (375 ML)

We use this classic dressing for our modern take on Caesar salad made with kale (page 62). It has also become a dipping sauce for our pizza crust, which then led customers to order it on the side with their French fries. White anchovies are pickled, as opposed to salted brown anchovies. We prefer the fresh tang of the white anchovies.

1. In a blender, combine the egg yolks, garlic, anchovies, and mustard. Purée well on medium speed.

2. With the blender on slow speed, slowly add the canola oil in a thin, steady stream.

3. Add Parmesan, lemon juice, hot sauce, salt, and pepper. Blend until smooth and homogenous.

4. Store in an airtight container, refrigerated, for up to 2 weeks.

2 egg yolks

1 clove garlic

4 anchovy fillets (we use white anchovies)

1½ teaspoons (7 mL) Dijon mustard

1 cup (250 mL) canola oil

⅓ cup (75 mL) grated Parmesan cheese

1 tablespoon (15 mL) freshly squeezed lemon juice

½ teaspoon (2 mL) JC's Hot Sauce (page 263), or store-bought

¼ teaspoon (1 mL) kosher salt

¼ teaspoon (1 mL) freshly ground pepper

MISO DRESSING

MAKES ¾ CUP (175 ML)

We love adding this exotic dressing to all kinds of dishes. Miso is packed full of the elusive "umami" taste, salty and sweet. Try it with the Shaved Fennel and Crab Salad (page 54) or Spicy Lentil, Wild Rice, and Orzo Salad (page 71).

1. In a small bowl, whisk together the canola oil, rice vinegar, mirin, miso paste, ginger, sesame oil, garlic, and cayenne. Season with salt and pepper.

2. Store in an airtight container, refrigerated, for up to 2 weeks.

3 tablespoons (45 mL) canola oil

2 tablespoons (30 mL) unseasoned rice vinegar

1 tablespoon (15 mL) mirin (sweet rice wine)

1 tablespoon (15 mL) miso paste

½ teaspoon (2 mL) minced fresh ginger

¼ teaspoon (1 mL) sesame oil

1 clove garlic, minced

Pinch of cayenne pepper

Kosher salt and freshly ground pepper

BASIC MAYONNAISE

MAKES 1 CUP (250 ML)

Nothing beats homemade mayonnaise, and it's so easy to make. We use it in several of our dressings and sauces, in salads and sandwiches. Of course, store-bought mayonnaise can be used in any of our recipes if you are pressed for time, but we encourage you make your own. It's a hundred times better.

---

1 clove garlic, chopped
¼ teaspoon (1 mL) kosher salt
2 large egg yolks
1 teaspoon (5 mL) Dijon mustard
1 cup (250 mL) canola oil
1 tablespoon (15 mL) freshly squeezed
  lemon juice

1. Using a mortar and pestle, mash the garlic with the salt to form a paste-like consistency. Stir in the egg yolks and mustard.

2. Whisk in the canola oil, a few drops at a time to begin with, mashing and stirring slowly until well combined and emulsified. Take your time with this; if the oil is added too quickly, the mayo can split and you will have to start all over again. Once about half the oil has been incorporated, you can start to add the oil in a thin, steady stream, whisking constantly. If, halfway through, the mayonnaise is too thick, add 1 tablespoon (15 mL) water to loosen it. Stir in the lemon juice.

3. Store in an airtight container, refrigerated, for up to 2 weeks.

CHIPOTLE MAYONNAISE

MAKES 1 CUP (250 ML)

This mayonnaise is kicked up a notch by the smoky chipotle pepper, which is a jalapeño pepper that has been smoked and dried. We use it on our Avocado, Tomato, Chicken, and Bacon Sandwich (page 124), but don't shy away from using it as a spread on burgers or a dip for pizza crust.

---

2 chipotle peppers in adobo sauce,
  minced
1 cup (250 mL) Basic Mayonnaise (recipe
  above) or store-bought
1 teaspoon (5 mL) freshly ground pepper

1. In a small bowl, whisk together the chipotle peppers, Basic Mayonnaise, and pepper.

2. Store in an airtight container, refrigerated, for up to 2 weeks.

THAI CHILI MAYONNAISE

Mayonnaise is one of what chefs call the "mother sauces," basic sauces that can be modified in endless ways to suit your needs. This Thai version is hot and zesty, which makes it a fun pairing with fried seafood like our Fried Calamari (page 99), or on burgers. (Shown on page 247.)

1 cup (250 mL) Basic Mayonnaise (page 246) or store-bought
2 tablespoons (30 mL) Thai fish sauce
1 teaspoon (5 mL) lightly packed brown sugar
1 teaspoon (5 mL) red chili flakes
½ teaspoon (2 mL) minced lemongrass, tender inner part of the stalk
1 clove garlic, minced
Grated zest and juice of 1 lime

1. In a small bowl, combine the Basic Mayonnaise, fish sauce, brown sugar, chili flakes, lemongrass, garlic, and lime zest and juice; whisk well.

2. Store in an airtight container, refrigerated, for up to 5 days.

SAFFRON MAYONNAISE

Saffron mayonnaise goes particularly well with shellfish, tomatoes, and lamb. We often serve this with Fried Calamari (page 99) or our Lamb Burger (page 116). (Shown on page 247.)

Pinch of saffron threads
1 cup (250 mL) Basic Mayonnaise (page 246) or store-bought
1 clove garlic, minced

1. Add the saffron threads to 1 tablespoon (15 mL) warm water and let infuse for 15 minutes.

2. In a small bowl, whisk together the Basic Mayonnaise, saffron threads, water, and garlic.

3. Store in an airtight container, refrigerated, for up to 5 days.

BASIL AND PINE NUT MAYONNAISE

MAKES 1 CUP (250 ML)

This mayonnaise goes well with grilled salmon or a bacon, lettuce, and tomato sandwich. Pine nuts can be expensive, so if you prefer, substitute blanched almonds in this recipe. (Shown on page 247).

1. In a small bowl, whisk together the Basic Mayonnaise, basil, pine nuts, and pepper.

2. Store in an airtight container, refrigerated, for up to 1 week.

1 cup (250 mL) Basic Mayonnaise (page 246) or store-bought
1 cup (250 mL) tightly packed fresh basil leaves, finely minced
1 tablespoon (15 mL) pine nuts, toasted and chopped
1 teaspoon (5 mL) freshly ground pepper

TRUFFLE MAYONNAISE

MAKES 1 CUP (250 ML)

Truffle mayonnaise loves Parmesan cheese and French fries. We serve truffle Parmesan fries by the truckload each year. People just can't get enough; we think it is because the earthy truffles are very exotic tasting in something so pedestrian as fries—and that's totally understandable! (Shown on page 249.)

1. In a small bowl, whisk together the Basic Mayonnaise, truffle oil, and pepper.

2. Store in an airtight container, refrigerated, for up to 1 week.

1 cup (250 mL) Basic Mayonnaise (page 246) or store-bought
2 teaspoons (10 mL) white truffle oil
1 teaspoon (5 mL) freshly ground pepper

MASTER BRINE

MAKES 2 CUPS (500 ML)

Brining helps retain moisture in meat during cooking and deeply seasons the meat for flavourful and juicy results. We use it a lot with pork and chicken, such as in our Pork Chops with Sage and Balsamic Vinegar (page 184), Buttermilk Fried Chicken (page 171), and Porchetta Sandwich (page 119).

2 cups (500 mL) water
½ cup (125 mL) kosher salt
2 cups (500 mL) ice
2 bay leaves
4 fresh sage leaves
4 cloves garlic, smashed
1 lemon, halved

1. Combine the water and salt in a small saucepan and bring to a boil over high heat. Cover, remove from the heat, and let sit for 10 minutes.

2. Put the ice in a bowl. Pour the brine over the ice. Stir until the ice is melted. Add the bay leaves, sage, garlic, and lemon halves. Let cool.

3. Store, covered and refrigerated, for up to 1 week.

CARAMELIZED ONIONS

MAKES 1½ CUPS (375 ML)

Caramelizing is a easy way to change the nature of onions. As onions slowly cook, their sugars begin to caramelize, turning them sweet and smoky. Serve caramelized onions on steaks (page 172) or roast chicken (page 167). They add a real depth of flavour to our Tomato, Goat Cheese, and Caramelized Onion Tartine (page 132); Apple Bacon Pizza (page 143); The Rob Pizza (page 154); and Mac and Cheese (page 189).

¼ cup (60 mL) olive oil
4 medium white onions, thinly sliced
2 tablespoons (30 mL) chopped fresh thyme
Kosher salt and freshly ground pepper

1. Heat the olive oil in a medium skillet over high heat. Add the onions and stir vigorously to avoid burning. Reduce the heat to medium. Add the thyme and season with salt and pepper. Continue to cook slowly, stirring occasionally, until the onions are soft and have taken on a deep brown colour, about 30 minutes. Let cool.

2. Store, covered and refrigerated, for up to 1 week.

CHIPOTLE BLACK BEANS

MAKES 2½ CUPS (625 ML)

Black beans are so healthy, and they are a smart addition to any meal.
We use these chipotle back beans in our Taco Salad (page 79).

1. Heat the canola oil in a medium skillet over high heat. Reduce the heat to medium. Add the onions and garlic and cook, stirring occasionally, until the onions are translucent and tender, about 10 minutes.

2. Add the beans and chipotle peppers, stir well, and simmer for about 8 minutes, until hot and fragrant.

3. Use immediately or let cool, then cover and refrigerate for up to 2 weeks.

3 tablespoons (45 mL) canola oil
1 cup (250 mL) minced white onion
2 cloves garlic
1 can (15 ounces/425 g) black beans, drained and rinsed
1 tablespoon (15 mL) chipotle peppers in adobo sauce, minced
Kosher salt and freshly ground pepper

CRISPY QUINOA

We use red quinoa for this crispy garnish, but you can use white or black if you like. It adds a nice crunch when served on porridge or any salad or used as a crust for roasted fish.

½ cup (125 mL) red quinoa, rinsed
2 cups (500 mL) water
3 tablespoons (45 mL) canola oil

1. In a small saucepan, combine the quinoa and water and bring to a boil. Reduce the heat to a simmer and cook, covered, for 10 to 12 minutes or until the quinoa is tender to the bite. Remove from the heat and let stand, covered, for 5 minutes. Drain, if needed, and spread on a plate to cool.

2. Heat the canola oil In a medium skillet over medium-high heat. Carefully add the cooled quinoa. Cook, stirring occasionally, until golden brown, about 5 to 6 minutes. Drain on a plate lined with paper towel. Let cool.

3. Store in an airtight container, refrigerated, for up to 2 days.

GARLIC CONFIT

MAKES ¾ CUP (175 ML)

Gently poaching garlic in olive oil mellows its astringency. We use this garlic most famously on the Vampire Slayer Pizza (page 157), but the oil is equally delicious on toast, in mayonnaise, and drizzled on soup.

---

1. Preheat the oven to 275°F (140°C).

2. Place the garlic cloves, thyme, and bay leaf in a small saucepan and pour in the olive oil. The oil should just cover the garlic. Over medium heat, bring the oil to just a hint of a simmer. Cover and cook in the oven for 1 hour. Check now and again to be sure the oil is not simmering. You want to poach the garlic, not simmer it. Remove from the oven and let cool completely.

3. Store in an airtight container, refrigerated, for up to 5 days.

4 heads garlic, cloves separated and peeled
5 sprigs fresh thyme
1 bay leaf
1 cup (250 mL) olive oil

CHILI CONFIT

MAKES 1 CUP (250 ML)

This condiment can be used on most anything. It has become a fixture in our home refrigerators for burgers, sandwiches, and on the side of roast chicken. The by-product is a chili oil that can be drizzled on just about anything lucky enough to receive it.

---

1. Combine the chilies, garlic, ginger, water, olive oil, sugar, and salt in a high-speed blender and purée to a coarse paste.

2. Heat a small saucepan over medium-high heat. Add the chili paste and fry for 8 minutes, stirring often. Remove from the heat and let cool.

3. Store, covered and refrigerated, for up to 1 week.

8 fresh long red chilies, seeded and coarsely chopped
8 cloves garlic
½ cup (125 mL) peeled and chopped fresh ginger
½ cup (125 mL) water
¼ cup (60 mL) olive oil
2 tablespoons (30 mL) sugar
½ teaspoon (2 mL) kosher salt

QUICK PICKLES

MAKES 2 CUPS (500 ML) · REQUIRES TIME FOR PREP

Pickling vegetables is so easy. Cucumbers and shallots are the vegetables that we pickle the most. Other veggies that pickle well when cut thin are beets, cauliflower, mushrooms, ramps, green onions, fennel, napa cabbage, cherry tomatoes, carrots, and pearl onions. You can use this brine either hot or cold. Enjoy Quick Pickled Cucumbers with our Quinoa Super-Star Veggie Burger (page 115) and Quick Pickled Shallots with the Umami Burger (page 112).

Pickle Brine

2 cups (500 mL) boiling water

1 cup (250 mL) unseasoned rice vinegar

6 tablespoons (90 mL) sugar

2 teaspoons (10 mL) kosher salt

2 sprigs fresh thyme

5 whole black peppercorns

¼ teaspoon (1 mL) red chili flakes

1. In a medium bowl, combine the boiling water, rice vinegar, sugar, and salt. Whisk until the salt and sugar are dissolved. Add the thyme, peppercorns, and chili flakes.

QUICK PICKLED CUCUMBER

1 cup (250 mL) cucumber sliced in coins

1. Place the cucumber in a small bowl. Pour the Pickle Brine over the cucumber, cover, and refrigerate. You can eat these pickles after 1 hour, but they will taste even better after 1 or 2 days.

QUICK PICKLED SHALLOTS

1 cup (250 mL) shallots cut into ⅛-inch (3 mm) rings

1. Place the shallots in a small bowl. Pour the Pickle Brine over the shallots, cover, and refrigerate. You can eat these pickles after 1 hour, but they will taste even better after 1 or 2 days.

GREEN OLIVE TAPENADE

MAKES 1 CUP (250 ML)

We prefer using green olives for tapenade rather than the traditional black olives. Green olives, to our tastes, have a herbaceous flavour that sings with lamb or fish. We use this tapenade for our Roasted Lamb Shoulder (page 179), and it also goes well with our Fried Calamari (page 99).

1. In a food processor, combine the olives, parsley, pine nuts, chili flakes, olive oil, water, and lemon juice. Process until smooth.

2. Store, covered and refrigerated, for up to 2 weeks.

1 cup (250 mL) green olives, pitted (we use picholine)

¼ cup (60 mL) chopped fresh flat-leaf parsley

2 tablespoons (30 mL) pine nuts, toasted

¼ teaspoon (1 mL) red chili flakes

3 tablespoons (45 mL) olive oil

1 tablespoon (15 mL) water

Juice of 1 lemon

GUACAMOLE

MAKES 1½ CUPS (375 ML)

The trend of Taco Tuesday has been an on-again, off-again love affair since we opened our restaurant. But our love of fresh guacamole has remained a constant throughout this tumultuous relationship. The keys to guacamole are to use ripe avocados and to serve just after making. This is perfect in our Taco Salad (page 79)!

2 tablespoons (30 mL) minced white onion
1 tablespoon (15 mL) seeded and minced jalapeño pepper
½ teaspoon (2 mL) kosher salt
¼ cup (60 mL) chopped fresh cilantro, divided
2 large ripe Hass avocados, halved and pitted
Juice of 2 limes

1. Using a mortar and pestle, mash together the onion, jalapeño, salt, and 2 tablespoons (30 mL) of the cilantro to make a paste. If you don't have a mortar and pestle, simply combine the ingredients in a medium bowl.

2. Using a knife, cut the flesh of the avocado halves in a crosshatch pattern, then scoop it out with a spoon into the mortar. Mix well. Add the remaining 2 tablespoons (30 mL) cilantro and the lime juice. Mash coarsely with a fork.

3. Serve immediately or refrigerate, covered, for up to 2 days.

SALSA VERDE

MAKES 1 CUP (250 ML)

Salsa Verde is a rich, bright-tasting sauce traditionally made with a mortar and pestle, but we've sped things up with the food processor. Perfect for Tomato Soup with Fried Chickpeas (page 39), Campfire-Style Rainbow Trout (page 196), and our Porchetta Sandwich (page 119).

---

1. In a food processor, combine the parsley, capers, and garlic. Pulse for about 1 minute to combine.

2. With the processor running, add the olive oil in an even stream, followed by the lemon zest and juice. Add the chili flakes and pulse to combine. Season with salt and pepper.

3. Cover and refrigerate for up to 2 weeks.

4 cups (1 L) fresh flat-leaf parsley leaves, chopped
¼ cup (60 mL) drained capers
1 clove garlic, chopped
½ cup (125 mL) extra-virgin olive oil
Grated zest and juice of ½ lemon
1½ teaspoons (7 mL) red chili flakes
Kosher salt and freshly ground pepper

SALSA ROSA

MAKES 2 CUPS (500 ML)

This is so much better than store-bought salsa—incomparable, actually. Now you can be in charge of how hot your salsa is and what type of herbs you would like to use. We serve this with fried corn chips, on top of Tomato Soup with Fried Chickpeas (page 39), and on our Porchetta Sandwich (page 119).

---

1. Place the onion in a small bowl of ice water and let sit while you prepare the rest of the ingredients. This will leach out any harshness of the raw onion. Drain the onion and pat dry with paper towels.

2. In a medium bowl, combine the onions, tomatoes, jalapeño, cilantro, olive oil, and lime juice; stir well. Season with salt and pepper. Serve immediately.

½ cup (125 mL) diced white onion
2 ripe tomatoes, seeded and diced
½ jalapeño pepper, seeded and minced
¼ cup (60 mL) chopped fresh cilantro
2 tablespoons (30 mL) olive oil
Juice of 2 limes
Kosher salt and freshly ground pepper

JALAPEÑO PESTO

Our bakers spread this pesto on bread and top with cheddar cheese for a kicked-up version of a cheese melt. We also use it in our Quinoa, Chickpea, and Black Bean Salad (page 67).

4 medium jalapeño peppers, seeded and coarsely chopped
2 cloves garlic, coarsely chopped
¼ cup (60 mL) raw sunflower seeds
½ cup (125 mL) extra-virgin olive oil
¼ cup (60 mL) grated Parmesan cheese
½ cup (125 mL) chopped fresh flat-leaf parsley
Juice of 1 lemon
Kosher salt

1. Place the jalapeños and garlic in a food processor and pulse for 30 seconds. Add the sunflower seeds and pulse for 30 seconds. Scrape down the sides of the bowl.

2. Add the olive oil and process for 15 seconds. Add the Parmesan and pulse until combined.

3. Add the parsley and lemon juice; process until smooth. Season with salt.

4. Serve immediately or refrigerate, covered, for up to 1 week.

TZATZIKI SAUCE

This versatile sauce serves us well as a party dip or spread on many sandwiches. Serve it with grilled kebabs in the summer or, as we do, on our Quinoa Super-Star Veggie Burger (page 115).

¼ cup (60 mL) coarsely shredded unpeeled, seeded cucumber
½ cup (125 mL) plain full-fat yogurt
¼ cup (60 mL) sour cream
1 clove garlic, minced
1 tablespoon (15 mL) minced fresh dill
1 tablespoon (15 mL) freshly squeezed lemon juice
Kosher salt

1. In a small bowl, combine the cucumber, yogurt, sour cream, garlic, dill, and lemon juice; mix well until smooth. Season with salt.

2. Serve immediately or refrigerate, covered, for up to 1 week.

WHITE SAUCE

MAKES 4 CUPS (1 L)

This is a classic béchamel sauce: milk infused with onion and thickened with flour and butter.
We use this as the base for our Mac and Cheese (page 189) and as the sauce on a few of our pizzas,
such as the Vampire Slayer Pizza (page 157).

1. Heat the milk and onions in a medium saucepan over medium heat until the milk comes to a bare simmer. Simmer for 10 minutes.

2. In a separate medium saucepan, melt the butter over medium heat. Add the flour and stir constantly until the flour has absorbed all the butter. Continue to cook, stirring, for 10 minutes, making sure the flour mixture does not brown.

3. Strain the milk into the hot flour mixture. Increase the heat to medium-high and whisk vigorously to break up any lumps. Bring to a boil, whisking frequently. The sauce will thicken once it begins to boil. Once thickened, remove from the heat and stir in the salt and nutmeg. Cool to room temperature before using. Can be made ahead up to 1 week, then covered and refrigerated.

4 cups (1 L) whole milk
½ small white onion, chopped
4 tablespoons (60 mL) unsalted butter
¼ cup (60 mL) all-purpose flour
1 teaspoon (5 mL) kosher salt
Pinch of nutmeg

RED SAUCE

MAKES 4 CUPS (1 L)

Our biggest fear about opening a pizzeria was making the red sauce. We used to slowly cook tomato sauce for
hours, and every once in a while a batch would burn. After trial and error we decided that the sauce can cook on
the pizza! No cook, no burn, no problem! We have found that this sauce is fresh and flavourful, and it has become
our kitchen workhorse for pastas, on pizzas, and in our Crispy Eggplant Melt (page 127).

1. In a large bowl, combine the tomatoes, water, basil, sugar, salt, and chili flakes. Stir well.

2. Store, covered and refrigerated, for up to 2 weeks.

4 cups (1 L) canned tomatoes, crushed
   by hand
¼ cup (60 mL) water
2 teaspoons (10 mL) dried basil
2 teaspoons (10 mL) sugar
2 teaspoons (10 mL) kosher salt
1 teaspoon (5 mL) red chili flakes

ROMESCO SAUCE

MAKES 4 CUPS (1 L)

Romesco sauce is our all-time favourite sauce. We love everything about it—the garlic, the fried bread, the nutty almonds. It is simply perfect. The trick is frying the bread in good oil, then adding the garlic for extra flavour. If you're short on time, it's okay to use store-bought roasted peppers. This sauce goes very well with chicken and fish. Try it with our Fried Chicken Sandwich (page 128) or Campfire-Style Rainbow Trout (page 196).

---

5 sweet red peppers
1¼ cups (300 mL) extra-virgin olive oil, divided
1 slice artisanal white bread, about 1 inch (2.5 cm) thick
2 cloves garlic, minced
1 medium tomato, cored, seeded, and chopped
⅓ cup (75 mL) slivered raw almonds
1 tablespoon (15 mL) minced fresh flat-leaf parsley
1 tablespoon (15 mL) sherry vinegar
Juice of 1 lemon
Kosher salt and freshly cracked pepper

1. Preheat a grill or broiler to high. Grill the red peppers, turning often with tongs, until blistered and blackened on all sides, about 15 minutes. Alternatively, roast the peppers directly over the stovetop flame of a gas oven. Transfer to a large bowl, cover with plastic wrap, and let steam for 20 minutes. Peel the peppers and chop them into ½-inch (1 cm) pieces. Place in a food processor.

2. In a medium skillet, heat ¼ cup (60 mL) of the olive oil over medium heat. Add the bread and fry, turning a few times, until golden brown on both sides, about 5 minutes. Break into 2 or 3 pieces and add to the food processor.

3. Return the skillet to medium heat. Add the garlic, tomato, and almonds; cook, stirring a few times, until the juices have evaporated, about 2 minutes. Scrape the mixture into the food processor.

4. Add the parsley, sherry vinegar, lemon juice, and the remaining 1 cup (250 mL) olive oil. Purée until smooth. Season with salt and pepper.

5. Store, covered and refrigerated, for up to 2 weeks.

BUTTER CHICKEN SAUCE

MAKES 2 CUPS (500 ML)

Butter chicken is the gentle ambassador of Indian food. We love how well it works on our Pizza Dough (page 139),
which is very similar to naan bread. Be sure to avoid any spice blend labelled "curry."
Garam masala is the superior option and is readily available in grocery stores.

1. Heat the canola oil in a medium saucepan over high
   heat. Reduce the heat to medium and add the onions,
   garlic, garam masala, paprika, cinnamon, and salt. Cook,
   stirring occasionally, until the onions are soft, about
   10 minutes.

2. Stir in the tomatoes and cook for another 5 minutes.

3. Add the White Sauce and butter. Stir well until the butter
   melts. Remove from the heat.

4. Use immediately or let cool, then cover and refrigerate
   for up to 2 weeks.

¼ cup (60 mL) canola oil
1 cup (250 mL) minced onion
3 cloves garlic, minced
2 tablespoons (30 mL) garam masala
2 teaspoons (10 mL) hot paprika
¼ teaspoon (1 mL) cinnamon
2 teaspoons (10 mL) kosher salt
1 cup (250 mL) canned crushed tomatoes
1 cup (250 mL) White Sauce (page 259)
2 tablespoons (30 mL) unsalted butter

JC'S BBQ SAUCE

MAKES 2 CUPS (500 ML)

At one point in our careers, making barbecue sauce from scratch seemed like a waste of time. We were happy with using our favourite store-bought sauce. Then, as we started to explore southern barbecue, it became clear that our own recipe was a must. And so we developed this tangy, hot, thin barbecue sauce in the North Carolina style. Use this sauce on our Overnight BBQ Brisket (page 183) or any grilled steak or chicken.

1. In a medium skillet, heat the bacon fat over high heat. Add the onions and chipotle and cook, stirring frequently, until charred, about 15 minutes.

2. Add the ketchup, rice vinegar, water, paprika, salt, and pepper. Simmer, stirring frequently, for 10 minutes, to bring all the flavours together. If you want a smooth sauce, allow to cool and purée in a blender on high speed for 3 minutes.

3. Store, covered and refrigerated, for up to 1 week.

2 tablespoons (30 mL) bacon fat or canola oil

1 Vidalia onion, minced

2 chipotle peppers in adobo sauce, minced

2 cups (500 mL) ketchup

½ cup (125 mL) unseasoned rice vinegar

½ cup (125 mL) water

1 teaspoon (5 mL) smoked paprika

1 teaspoon (5 mL) kosher salt

1 teaspoon (5 mL) freshly ground pepper

JC'S HOT SAUCE

MAKES 2 CUPS (500 ML)

Say goodbye to Sriracha and make your own hot sauce. The depth of flavour you can achieve at home is amazing. When we make hot sauce, we leave the seeds in the chilies—it's got to be hot! Be sure to refrigerate the sauce, as it will ferment at room temperature, potentially causing the lid to pop off. We use this hot sauce in our Fried Chicken Sandwich (page 128) and in our Caesar Salad Dressing (page 245).

1. In a large skillet, heat the oil until near the smoking point. Add the habanero, jalapeño, poblano, and sweet red peppers and cook, stirring occasionally, until fork-tender and charred, about 15 minutes. Remove from the heat and let cool.

2. Place the roasted peppers in a blender and add the salt, sugar and rice vinegar, sugar, and salt. Purée on high speed for 3 minutes. Adjust the sweetness or seasoning to your taste.

3. Store, covered and refrigerated, for up to 2 weeks.

1 tablespoon (15 mL) canola oil

4 habanero chilies, stemmed

6 jalapeño peppers, stemmed and halved lengthwise

1 poblano chili, chopped

4 sweet red peppers, halved and seeded

1½ cups (375 mL) unseasoned rice vinegar

4 teaspoons (20 mL) sugar

2 teaspoons (10 mL) kosher salt

JC'S BURGER SAUCE

MAKES 1 CUP (250 ML)

What a brilliant idea to combine all the condiments that go on our Cheese Burger (page 111) in one bottle. Jeff thought he was a genius to invent it, until a cook told him it's basically Thousand Island Dressing. Still, nothing beats this homemade version!

½ cup (125 mL) Basic Mayonnaise (page 246) or store-bought
½ cup (125 mL) ketchup
¼ cup (60 mL) yellow mustard
¼ cup (60 mL) sweet pickle relish
1 tablespoon (15 mL) hot sauce
1 teaspoon (5 mL) pepper
1 teaspoon (5 mL) white wine vinegar

1. In a small bowl, combine the Basic Mayonnaise, ketchup, mustard, relish, hot sauce, pepper, and vinegar. Stir well.

2. Store, covered and refrigerated, for up to 2 weeks.

UMAMI SAUCE

MAKES 1 CUP (250 ML)

Umami flavour is all the rage, and for good reason. We add this to our Crispy Brussels Sprouts (page 96) and of course the Umami Burger (page 112).

½ cup (125 mL) hoisin sauce
½ cup (125 mL) your favourite barbecue sauce
1 teaspoon (5 mL) white truffle oil

1. In a small bowl, combine the hoisin sauce, barbecue sauce, and truffle oil. Stir well.

2. Store, covered and refrigerated, for up to 2 weeks.

PIRI PIRI DRY RUB

MAKES ¼ CUP (60 ML)

We love this spice blend! Spicy with a hint of citrus, made-from-scratch Piri Piri is head and shoulders above any store-bought version. Use it on chicken, pork, fish, roasted cauliflower, and of course our Piri Piri Baby Back Ribs (page 176).

1. In a small bowl, combine the paprika, salt, oregano, ginger, cardamom, garlic powder, onion powder, cayenne, sugar, lemon zest, and lime zest. Stir well.

2. Store, covered and refrigerated, for up to 1 month.

1 tablespoon (15 mL) hot paprika
2 teaspoons (10 mL) kosher salt
1 teaspoon (5 mL) dried oregano
1 teaspoon (5 mL) ground ginger
1 teaspoon (5 mL) ground cardamom
1 teaspoon (5 mL) garlic powder
1 teaspoon (5 mL) onion powder
½ teaspoon (2 mL) cayenne pepper
½ teaspoon (2 mL) sugar
Zest of 1 lemon, minced
Zest of 1 lime, minced

ZA'ATAR SPICE BLEND

MAKES ½ CUP (125 ML)

Za'atar is a Middle Eastern spice mix that adds a mysteriously tangy, herb-forward flavour to any ho-hum dish. Use it in salads and on bread, chicken, and seafood. You can sprinkle it on our Creamy Hummus with Fried Chickpeas (page 103) and Delicata Squash with Sprouted Chickpeas (page 192).

1. In a small bowl, combine the sumac, thyme, marjoram, basil, sesame seeds, and salt.

2. Store, covered and refrigerated, for up to 2 weeks.

¼ cup (60 mL) ground sumac
2 tablespoons (30 mL) chopped fresh thyme
2 tablespoons (30 mL) dried marjoram
2 tablespoons (30 mL) dried basil
1 tablespoon (15 mL) sesame seeds, toasted
1 teaspoon (5 mL) kosher salt

VADOUVAN SPICE BLEND

MAKES 1 CUP (250 ML)

Making up curry spice blends from scratch may seem daunting, but we feel it is totally worth the effort. The flavours really sing, and when your guests notice the difference, you'll be bursting with pride. Vadouvan blend is distinctive: there's a bit of French fusion with the dried fried onions. We love it and make it the star in our French Carrot Salad (page 72), but you'll end up adding it to all sorts of dishes. Make up extra and give some away as gifts. Dried fried onions and garlic and fresh curry leaves are available at South Asian and Asian markets.

---

2 tablespoons (30 mL) coriander seeds

2 teaspoons (10 mL) cumin seeds

2 teaspoons (10 mL) fenugreek seeds

13 small fresh curry leaves, cut into thin strips

1 tablespoon (15 mL) minced fresh ginger

⅓ cup (75 mL) dried fried onions

2 tablespoons (30 mL) dried fried garlic

2 tablespoons (30 mL) Madras curry powder

1 tablespoon (15 mL) kosher salt

2 teaspoons (10 mL) yellow mustard seeds

2 teaspoons (10 mL) hot paprika

1½ teaspoons (7 mL) red chilli flakes

1 teaspoon (5 mL) ground cardamom

½ teaspoon (2 mL) freshly grated nutmeg

¼ teaspoon (1 mL) ground cloves

¼ teaspoon (1 mL) cayenne pepper

1. First toast the seeds. Heat a medium skillet over medium heat. Add the coriander, cumin, and fenugreek seeds and stir (or shake the pan). After a minute, they will start to release their aroma and begin to crackle. Continue to toast the spices a few more minutes, stirring and watching them closely—make sure they don't burn. The spices should smell nutty and sweet. Grind in a spice grinder to a fine powder.

2. In a small bowl, combine the ground toasted seeds, curry leaves, ginger, dried fried onions, dried fried garlic, curry powder, salt, mustard seeds, paprika, chili flakes, cardamom, nutmeg, cloves, and cayenne. Stir well

3. Store in an airtight container, refrigerated, for up to 1 month or in the freezer for up to 3 months.

ACKNOWLEDGEMENTS

Over the years we have worked with a long list of staff, customers, suppliers, and colleagues. This beautiful book you hold in your hands is a journal of sorts, full of lessons we have learned from working with exceptional people.

We would like to thank our families:

Jeff—Julie, Kane, Finn, and Brenda.

Bettina—Tom, Eleanor, Bruce, and Echo.

We would like to thank our very talented team at Bread Bar: Erin Schiestel (Pastry Chef), Denise Frenette, Rosie Vandenbos, Denique Davidson, Katrina Vandenberg, our current chefs Cameron Bell and Mike Spitzig, and past chef Manny Ferreira. The food they put out day after day is mind-boggling, both in quantity and quality. No one works harder than cooks!

Thank you, as well, to the front-of-house team, Maria Guarnieri, Holly Gibb, Katie Shewen, Jenn Badley, Mark Dyer, Samantha Clark, and Ben Ragetlie, whose genuine hospitality sets the stage for our customers to have a unique experience.

Thanks to our partners Aaron Ciancone and the Pearle Hospitality family for supporting our ideas. Jocelyn Maurice, Leanne Ciancone, Jill McGoey, Matthew Opferkuch, Heather Sinfield, Evan Baulch, and Sarah Kidd-Beres, much appreciated.

Earth to Table Farm team, Jennifer Evans, Kaoru Nagayama, Chris Bocz, Jessica McLean, and Rowena Cruz. No one works harder than farmers!

Food stylist Claire Stubbs and photographer Maya Visnyei. Thanks to these pros for the jaw-dropping shots of our food . . . seriously, you are that good. Jeff concedes he could not have done as well with his iPhone.

Andrea Magyar at Penguin Random House gave us the green light to work on our second cookbook (thank you!) and help us shape it into something we are terribly proud of (thank you again!).

For the second book in a row we need to thank Sarah Brohman. Sarah is a regular at Bread Bar, and we have watched her daughter grow from toddler to teen and always save a blueberry scone for her.

We are blessed to have a community of bona fide foodies at our fingertips. We put a call out for volunteers to help with recipe testing and were overwhelmed with eighty-plus responses. We chose twenty to help. Thanks to you all—Stephen Schormann, Jenn Badley, Calvin Sims, Mary Orr, Kathryn Lee, Taryn Aarssen, Tanja Roglic, Melanie Skriac, Nathalie Hughes, Lori Edwards, Megan Cherniak, Jenn Kotacka, Aaron Hodgson, Sarah Edwards, Anishka Saldanha, Michael Dean, Vince Salteri, Rianna Angemi, Donna Caprice, Joanne Hudspith, and Alex McKenzie, our recipe consultant.

INDEX